THE

Laughter and Tears

OF

CHILDREN

Marilyn Bonham

ABBEY PRESS

St. Meinrad, Indiana 47577

ABBEY PRESS

St. Meinrad, Indiana 47577

To My Husband

WHO HAS GIVEN OUR CHILDREN
THEIR WONDROUS LAUGHTER
AND TAKEN AWAY THEIR TEARS

Contents

Contents

I

Your Moment of Truth

IF YOUR CHILD could write a book about himself, about you, and your relationship to each other, it could very well be a book such as this. But since your child cannot, I shall try to write it for him. While I may not know *your* child, much of my professional life has been taken up in knowing and studying children like your own.

I am tempted to say at the very outset that if you begin to hear your own child talk through these pages, you are already one step ahead of most other parents. While the vast majority of us try to be loving and effective parents, many of us have somehow lost a crucial parental touch, a true insight into the inner world of our children.

These pages have a good deal to say about insight: insight into ourselves, into our children, and into the world about us. In the accepted sense of the term, one can pass for a "good" parent without such an understanding of the inner child. But once having gained it, a third dimension is added to parenthood. It helps bridge the parent-child relationship within which the child's emotional health can genuinely flourish. The laughter and tears of your child are in many ways a reflecting pool of the quality of life between you.

This book is concerned with the future, not the past. All too many parents only discover their failure to respond to the deeper issues of their chil-

dren's inner lives long after they are grown up.
By then, it is far too late. The regrets sear the
heart, but the process is irreversible. One-time opportunities are lost forever, and parent-child relationships can be no more reconstituted than scram-
bled eggs.

For the parent with the most stable of children,
a full awareness of the nature and symptoms of
emotional trouble is no less crucial than a ready
detection of an onset of chicken pox. One must
learn at least the principles of emotional illness in
order to know emotional health.

No discussion of your child's emotional life can
center on your child alone. You are forever on-
stage. At no other time have you been as much
exposed to advice as today. No self-respecting
magazine or newspaper can afford to be without
it. The advice is not always consistent, but it is
always available. Bookstores and libraries offer
similar guidance in longer versions. Our pediatri-
cians, too, form an increasingly authoritative
source of advice on the emotional life of your child.

And yet, this is the continuing enigma. With
all such counsel filling parents' eyes and ears in
such overabundance, we have never before had as
much mental illness, more emotionally disturbed
youngsters, a larger number of juvenile delinquents, or as many "alienated" young people. My
own child guidance clinic, as every other, is so
swamped by families seeking help that we cannot
possibly hope to cope with the throngs at our clinic
doors.

Since we cannot realistically expand the nation's
facilities to cope successfully with every child under a variety of emotional stresses, we had better
try to help prevent their occurrence in the first
place. A deeper understanding of what makes

your child behave as he does can have precisely
this end result. Many of the children under treatment today would not have needed psychiatric
treatment at all if full parental support and insight had been available some years before.

It is commonly assumed that emotionally disturbed children are ordinarily children of econom-
ically underprivileged families, broken homes, or
of the culturally deprived. While this is partly
true it is of interest to note that the children under
my treatment all live in Westchester County, one
of the most affluent sections of our nation. The
parents of the children I see tend to have inor-
dinately high incomes, a college education, and intelligence well above the national norm. There are
also thousands upon thousands of Westchester children in need of professional help who are not getting it. Facilities are totally inadequate, and parents, as parents everywhere, either deny the existence of a problem, or simply are unaware of it.

We also often observe the opposite phenomenon.
We see many parents each year who are concerned
about their children's behavior when they should
not be. Perfectly normal children do some strange
things in the process of growing up. These have
no long-term significance.

Many parents, while armed with an almost en-
cyclopedic expertise on chicken pox and dental
care, become hopelessly lost in even the simplest
of psychic processes which engage the developing
child. It is not necessary to analyze your child's
every move, but it is terribly important to recognize that the emotional life of your child requires
your own deep involvement and understanding. It
is true that his physical well-being is more apparent, more visible, and much more easily monitored.
It is vital, in short, for the parent to know what

constitutes *normal* behavior, before any abnormalities can be identified.

It is the curse of emotionally disturbed children that many of them can pass through childhood without a single sudden and acute event of abnormal behavior which would compel the parents, the school, or the community to take action. Troubled children often go undetected until they set fire to their school, hit another child into insensibility, or fail to complete the most basic of school assignments. Even in the most extreme cases, where a child kills a member of his family, or is hospitalized in a mental ward as a last resort, the common reaction of family and acquaintances is one of shocked disbelief that this could have happened to such an "obviously normal" child.

Children do not snap or crack overnight. Like a major disease, emotional illness often takes years from onset to its acute phase. The vast majority of troubled children can be helped. Such help, however, invariably is more successful in the early stages.

All too many children these days grow into adulthood with variably serious permanent emotional handicaps which their parents never knew existed. School and college guidance counselors and health services are filled with troubled children and young adults, much to the surprise and deep chagrin of a very large proportion of their parents.

Love of one's child is not enough. It is basic to all else, but it is not the only requisite for parenthood. The young child needs love, to be sure, but it is love with a special kind of insight into his special world which will feed his spirit and give him the psychic strength upon which he may build firm concepts of himself and life around him. Many parents somehow assume that their world and their child's is one and the same. They believe that whatever they may communicate, by action, by words, and by feeling, will be identically received.

The facts are otherwise. From the day of birth, your child is a separate and highly individualistic human being. Genetics have performed their vital function. What kind of human being your child will turn out to be is already in part determined. But your own influence on him—particularly in the first three or four years—will have a profoundly determining effect on your child's ability to relate successfully to himself, and the world in which he is to live.

The built-in hazard of describing human behavior is to lapse into generalizations which may apply to groups as a whole, but never to the individual. No two children are alike, and their emotional growth cannot be programmed on a computer. Nevertheless, this book largely parallels the chronological development of your child, since this is the most logical approach from the reader's point of view. Few parents need to be reminded, however, that extremely wide variations apply from one child to the next. While the psychological principles remain the same, few will ever apply at the same time to the same child.

Preceding the evaluation of children's emotionality by growth stages is a chapter which may help the parent define the organic and psychiatric origins of their child's emotional development. The psychic and physical aspects of human life are closely interwoven, relating to each other in cause and effect. These relationships deserve some exploration, so that the rest may be understood.

After detailed discussions of the various emotional age-stages follow several chapters on the specific problems of the withdrawn and the aggressive child, as well as a rather explicit exploration of crucial learning problems. Emotionally disturbed children will often manage reasonably well in the first years of life, only to be caught up in the structured demands of the school. Literally millions of children eventually become involved in some learning disorder. The schools have become increasingly one vast significant screening net, in which troubled children encounter their first acute failure to cope with life.

Parents who may wish to seek professional guidance and counseling for their children will find the last chapter a source of information on where help may be obtained. The final decision to seek help represents to any family a major commitment. Never is it an easy one to make. Having made it, however, the first hurdle is already left behind.

This book is primarily devoted to assuring parents that they are probably already better parents than they now think they are. Too many of us are already too guilt-ridden to make us successful parents in the full sense of the word. But the best of parents should also acknowledge the possible need for outside help. The child cannot ask for it. The decision must be made by mature and selfless adults. It is, significantly and lastingly, a parent's own Moment of Truth.

II

Nature and Nurture

IT COMES as an open surprise to many parents that a clinic pays a good deal of attention to the physical and neurological history of the disturbed child and his family. In my own clinic, the careful evaluation of a detailed three-page neurological questionnaire precedes any determination as to how the patient is to be treated. We look at the human being in totality because his physical and psychological aspects are so closely interwoven.

Complex relationships also exist between heredity and physical history. Many parents are often concerned with the organic aspects of emotional disorders. Mystified by their child's abnormal behavior, many parents view the physiological background and history as the underside of an iceberg —never seen, but always dangerous. They carry the unspoken fear that emotional disturbance may be deeply rooted in the child's parents, grandparents, or even earlier generations.

Other parents seem surprised at our suggestion that physical and hereditary factors can play a role in a particular emotional problem. There still exists a widely held impression that all physical illnesses are invariably physical in causation, and that all emotional problems are always due to some purely psychological cause. In truth, the line of demarcation is often vague and difficult to trace.

Multiple events of a psychological, physiological, neurological, as well as genetic nature impinge on each human being from the moment of his birth and, through his parents, long before. Modern psychiatry stands today at the threshold of vast new insights into the true causation and treatment of mental illness. Much of the credit for such recent advances goes not to psychiatry, but to important discoveries by biochemists, biologists, and geneticists. These discoveries are revolutionizing psychiatric treatment. A full one-third of all prescription drugs sold today are designed to treat the mind. The most serious cases of schizophrenia, of anxiety and depression, have shown remarkable improvement by the use of drug therapy. Indeed, drug therapy has significantly changed our thinking on the very nature of mental illness itself, and has proved a powerful aid in the treatment of psychoses. Unhappily, drugs have not yet helped us significantly in the treatment of neuroses.[1]

The dramatic use of new drugs illustrates how very significant are the connecting bonds between the physical and psychic parts of human nature. Since the introduction of tranquilizers in 1956, for example, there has been a substantial reduction in the number of mental patients in our hospitals. Dr. Nathan S. Kline of the Rockland New York State Hospital has estimated that since 1956, we have had a net decrease of 54,000 patients in mental wards. Without these new drugs, we would in the same period have had a net increase of 82,000 new hospitalized mental patients. Significantly, adds Dr. Kline, a minimum outlay of $3 billion would have been needed for the additional treatment and facilities. Thus the use of chemotherapy in the treatment of the mind represents one of the major medical revolutions of our time.

To parents who are only normally curious about the organic and hereditary aspects of their child's inner self, the recognition that these exceedingly complex relationships do exist and are powerfully interconnected seems sufficient and not particularly disturbing. But other parents scour their family tree, five generations back, to find some rationale for their child's odd behavior. Such dark visions cannot be scoffed at. It is easy enough to reassure a mother that her little girl's anxiety is due to the child's poor and uncorrected eyesight. It is quite another matter to discount the alarms of a hysterical mother who tells you that her husband's great-aunt died insane in some remote asylum. Nor is she consoled by being told that such secrets exist in most family closets. Some vaguely recalled family insanity makes the butt of a good family joke, but let the first hint of mental trouble arise here and now, and the family joke quickly turns to a gnawing fear that is only uttered behind closed doors. One can only wonder how dead are those memories of the seventeenth century when the mentally ill were generally thought to be inhabited by some demon or devil. Severe punishment or death was the usual treatment.

What ought we to know about the significance of hereditary factors? Parents want to know what, if any, genetic abnormalities may play a role in familial mental abnormalities. It is probable that even subtle genetic errors increase a person's susceptibility to emotional disturbance, although these, by themselves, do not trigger the problem. Genetic aberrations are evident in certain kinds of mental retardation, such as Mongolism, where the addition of an extra chromosome is recognized as a definite form of genetic error.

While there can be a direct relationship between hereditary genes and mental retardation, the precise role of heredity in an emerging mental disturbance is by no means clear. Still, we frequently face parental questions such as these: "Has my great-uncle's insanity brought on my child's anxiety attacks?" Or, to quote another, "Has my maternal grandfather's alcoholism anything to do with Billy's own insecurities?"

I am always quick to answer that we have no absolute evidence that neurotic illness can be inherited of itself. Hereditary factors may predispose a person in a given direction, but this is quite different from pointing an accusing finger at heredity itself. If insanity is indeed traceable to some earlier generation, it is well to remember that, if the truth were known, few families can point to a family tree totally free of such afflictions.

The Abbé Mendel discovered that hereditary characteristics are carried independently in both the male and female seed. When combined in the production of a new individual, these characteristics either reinforce or modify each other. The child retains the proper proportion of inherited characteristics of both the mother and the father, ready to be passed along to succeeding generations. As a rule, any faulty genetic hereditary factor is apt to remain recessive and likely to be outweighed by the more dominant and favorable characteristics of generations of reasonably normal, healthy stock.

Even where one of the parents suffers from a mental illness, such as schizophrenia or a severe neurosis, the chances of genetically transferring it to the child are not much greater than if both parents had been perfectly normal. However, while heredity may play an insignificant role in the event, the emotional development of a child of an emotionally disturbed parent is open to other dangers. These have to do with environment, not with heredity.

Heredity, in short, plays in most cases only a peripheral role in the context of our discussion. It must not become the focus of a family's obsessions with its past. Nothing can be done about heredity. Some parents, knowingly or not, take passive refuge in the immutable cloak of heredity, instead of helping themselves and their children solve their current problems.

Once parents are out of the woods of what one mother calls "the heredity bogeyman," one can begin to discuss the effect of heredity on the emotional health of the child in far more rational terms. Let us remember this: Two blue-eyed people may produce all blue-eyed children, but two people of exceptionally aggressive character will not necessarily produce a basically aggressive child. The color of an off-spring's eyes is far more easily determined than the particular nature of an individual's personality.

While constitutional factors such as tranquility or nervousness are sometimes transmitted by heredity, life's experiences shape these qualities into a thousand variations.

If the influence of heredity and the influence of the parent over the child's emotional life is compared, it is the environmental impact of the parent which must be considered predominant. Parents should never lull themselves into the belief that their child's obstinacy, his lack of sensitivity, or his bullying behavior are the result of inexorable heredity factors. The finger must unremittingly point to them. It is they who carry the ultimate responsibility as to how their young offspring are likely to turn out.

"Parents exercise a prodigious power over in-

dividual destinies," writes one authority in the
field. "It is they who bear the responsibility, in the
last resort, for the good or bad character, the
sound or defective development of their children.
That is, they ought to bear the responsibility if
only they were conscious of their power."[2]

Fear of one's past often dominates a family's
emotional life, and leaves emotional scars. For the
last two years, I have had in treatment a thirty-six
year old mother of four children, three of whom
have already been referred to my clinic for psychiatric treatment. Mrs. F.'s husband drinks heavily.
She lives in constant fear of his becoming an alcoholic like her father. She is convinced that she
will undoubtedly end up like her mother, and that
her children will meet a similar fate. Her fears
have mounted to such overriding proportions that
she frequently overreacts in her anxiety and
creates serious problems for herself as well as her
whole family.

This case illustrates to what an extent the fear
of an abnormal constitutional and hereditary past
can shape the whole family environment. Whether
it be a history of alcoholism, or another form of
disease, it can produce anxiety and great unhappiness. Just how each person suffering from any of
these torments feels about himself often lies at
the crux of any mental illness. It is in this inner
view of the human self to his or her outside world
in which we often find the clue to the treatment
of mental disease.

What about the organic damage and physical
deprivation and its effect on the mental health of
the individual? We see many thousands of newly
discovered emotionally ill children each year whose
basic reason for their condition goes back to some
trauma suffered shortly before, during, or after

birth. Among such prenatal, natal, and postnatal trauma we include infection, anoxemia (insufficient oxygen in the blood), chemical toxicity, excessive x-rays, forced labor and delivery, and a host of other possible complications of pregnancy and birth.

Thanks to modern medicine, we now have many thousands of babies who, only a few short years ago, could not have survived their precarious birth. But we have also become extremely aware of some of the continuing hazards of such births. Because we manage to save many more babies than ever before, we also see a steadily rising number of organically damaged children. Some suffer permanent defects of their cerebral functions or some neurological damage, with consequent dire effect on the child's emotional development. Insufficient or excessive use of oxygen by the newborn may cause serious problems, as can German measles during the mother's first trimester of pregnancy. Both may cause retardation in the newborn child, as may certain drugs, either directly or through side effects. The most dramatic illustration of this occurred in 1962, when the use of Thalidomide, a tranquilizer, was discovered to cause underdeveloped limbs in six thousand German babies, and sixteen babies in this country.

All of this is not to say that the hazards of birth are so pervading that complications such as these are either frequent or severe. But among emotionally disturbed children, such a medical history is frequent and significant. Four-year-old Karen is such a child. Her mother first brought her to my clinic because of the child's hyperactivity. The mother, being a very quiet and sensitive woman, found her child's behavior completely unmanageable. As we checked more closely into

Karen's medical past, we found that she had been born after prolonged and difficult labor. Forceps had had to be used, and our diagnostic study indicated diffuse brain damage.

Our treatment of Karen combined medication to slow down her exceedingly tense and overactive behavior, with therapy channeling her hyperactivity into more acceptable outlets, as well as helping Karen's mother understand her daughter's emotional problems.

A more complex case was seven-year-old David. He was referred because of his poor school performance. Like Karen, he was hyperactive and was given to severe temper tantrums. David was the oldest of three boys. His two brothers were born with a hare lip, a congenital birth defect.

Even though David appeared bright, he was unable, verbally or in writing, to express the ideas that flowed through his mind. Diffuse brain damage produced in David a maturational lag as well as some mild neurological problems, which continually caused a great deal of frustration. Frequent temper tantrums expressed these frustrations. His parents' incessant demands on him only increased his frustration and tension. The result was a very bad home environment.

David was quite typical in that he exhibited emotional problems which arose from organic difficulties of his own as well as those of his elders. David's mother was an epileptic. Her frequent falls and convulsions during her pregnancy had undoubtedly contributed to David's own neurological problems. Her labor was prolonged and difficult. Some members of the father's family also showed organic brain damage, even though the father himself appeared to be normal. But the fear of a hereditary problem remained.

Our treatment with David proceeded along several lines. First of all, we attempted to help his parents understand the true nature of his neurological handicaps. David's teacher and school authorities fully cooperated in patiently helping him integrate his slow school progress into our own schedule of therapy. Our therapy with David aimed at providing him with a warm and supportive mother figure. We also encouraged positive outlets for his abnormal behavior patterns which arose from his feelings of frustration and aggression.

So far as the emotional life of the handicapped child is concerned, we can go a long way toward helping him regain his emotional equilibrium by diverting his life energies and strengths around his particpular handicap. We can help him construct his life and his environment in such a manner that his abnormalities will sooner or later fade into acceptance and normalcy. What emerges then of significance to the afflicted child is a reconstruction of both functional as well as emotional abilities, and perhaps to substitute certain functions for some others, which, in time, may become indistinguishable and perfectly acceptable.

Parents should know that the hazards of neurological and other organic damage are being constantly reduced. Our advanced knowledge of psycho-physical relationships helps throw insights into the power of the mind to overcome and heal physical abnormalities. At the same time, the vast contribution of sound physical health to a rational emotional life is also fully recognized. But while the healing powers of medicine and psychiatry stand here revealed as unprecedented heights, both still bow to the child's most potent healer—the parent himself.

1 Psychosis is a more severe form of mental illness than neurosis. More common are neurotic persons, usually amenable to psychotherapy, who fail to adjust to internal and external stresses. This creates various forms of anxiety, expressed through depression, persistent fatigue, intellectual underachievement, detachment, somatic disorders, etc. Psychosis, which can be due to either physical or mental aberrations, usually results in a total inability to function and to adjust to life. Psychotherapy is occasionally helpful, and, increasingly, newer forms of drug therapy are being used.

2 *Early Years of Life*, Alice Balint, Basic Books, Inc., New York, 1954, pp. 128-129.

III

The First Year of Life: The Patterns Form

IN FEW PARTS of the world is the newborn child cared for as assiduously as in the United States. From the first moment of life, he is the beneficiary of the most modern pediatric care and technology. His development is marked by frequent checkups, three-in-one shots, growth and weight charts, premixed formulas, silver rattles, vaporizers, and last but not least, cribs with innerspring mattresses.

Yet, I often wonder if some babies in less blessed lands are not just a little better off in one very important way. Our babies' creature-comforts are so dazzlingly provided for that their emotional health only too often seems to take a back seat. In less affluent parts of the world, what the baby may lack in medical attention and baby-care manuals the mother may make up in an enveloping closeness to her child, which, in many American households, is rapidly becoming a lost art.

Let us not confuse the two: The mechanics of baby care are essential, but not the end-all. The little Polynesian child strapped to his mother's back, and a thousand miles from the nearest penicillin supply, will probably receive his essential emotional needs, while many a baby in our antiseptic nurseries, despite all the physical care lavished on him, will be denied that special care so vital to his development and happiness.

In my own clinical experience, I find all too many women making the tragic assumption that the physically well-cared-for baby is, almost by definition, also the happy baby. The assumption is also current that, if a choice has to be made, parental attention and love is far more decisive in the later years than in the *vegetable* existence of the newborn child.

Not too long ago, I was visited by a woman lawyer in her thirties. How soon after delivery of her child, she asked, could she return to her job? A nursemaid of twenty years' experience had already been engaged. When I suggested that she really ought to be home with her child, if at all possible, she exploded and stormed out of my office.

Today this attitude is more common than we like to admit. One mother who consulted me on the same point suggested that I was just a little old-fashioned. I am happy to be a little "old-fashioned" when I think of the many older children and adults walking about today with serious emotional scars, who were deprived of their mothers' precious love and attention during the years when it counted most: at the beginning of life.

It is a deceptive beginning: deceptive, because to feed and to burp a baby seems to be all he might expect. He cannot yet express all of his needs. He cannot tell you how much he craves for the warmth of his mother's body, for the security of her presence, for her soothing voice and her special touch. Where these are absent, the baby suffers. Perhaps in silence. But he suffers, and the deprivation will almost inevitably show up later on in life.

The first year of life, of course, is not an un-alloyed blessing. The glamor of a new baby in the house may soon wear a bit thin, especially at the end of a sleepless night. He will demand a great deal from both parents. This is very much a time of "give, give, give," and the love and attention will for a while go pretty much one way. But the outflow of this love and affection for the very young child is pure gold in the bank. A world of love and the constant security of parental proximity will give him a view of the world which is golden and generous and serene.

These early days between mother and child can be the most memorable and beautiful period imaginable. But only too often, for one reason or another, the mother denies herself one of the truly rare privileges of her life—to give her love unstintingly, and without limitation. This tiny human being's survival depends just as much on his mother's love and closeness as on his proper formula.

Why is the emotional care and feeding of the very young child so essential to the building of his emotional resources? Ample clinical evidence indicates that where there exists a total emotional deprivation for the infant, the physical consequences are frequently tragic and irreversible. Illegitimate children, deprived from the start of prenatal care and attention, tragically illustrate the case in point. Those who cannot be immediately placed with foster or adopted parents often show an early history of severe emotional as well as physical handicaps. Our child-caring institutions consider such cases almost routine. These babies do not gain weight, show difficulties in breathing, and remain unresponsive and listless. They give concern to the psychiatric worker as well as to the pediatrician.

Recognizing the serious emotional deprivation of these children, many advanced hospitals today provide volunteer mother services. Woman volunteers "mother" such children twice daily. Rocking and cradling these lonely babies, singing to them, stroking their heads softly stimulates a close human relationship, which unfortunately never quite replaces the genuine thing. Even so, these are the fortunate ones. Relatively few such babies receive this kind of care.

Unhappily, many of my own professional hours are spent treating the effects of legitimate children brought up in emotionally barren, and in a sense, illegitimate ways. These are usually the children of mothers who turn over virtually all mothering to a nursemaid, an elderly aunt, or a grandmother; or of mothers involved in bad marriages, of mothers divorced, or of absentee mothers, or just plain inadequate mothers who consider their obligations done when their child is fed and properly diapered.

To the detriment of the child, we usually see such emotionally deprived children long after the deprivation began, and often too late. If, somehow, we could reach the mother just before or after her child's birth, much needless damage could be prevented. Many highly intelligent mothers provide their offspring with everything except what they need most of all: a mother's insight into her baby's basic emotional hungers.

How then can a mother fulfill the baby's basic needs? A baby, we must remember, functions entirely on a feeling level. He can only *feel* how his mother relates to him. He cannot reason it out. He cannot rationalize his mother's affections. He cannot say to himself, "Mother didn't cuddle me tonight because she is having a quarrel with Daddy."

It bears repeating that for some months after his birth, the child is so incomplete physically and emotionally that he cannot function without his mother. His very survival depends on the adult world around him, and he is not at all convinced that it is a hospitable world.

The well-adjusted woman should never feel any inadequacy in being able to satisfy her baby's needs. Most mothers grow to know their child, both by instinct and by observation. Where they often fail is by judging the baby's behavior in adult terms. With the firstborn, of course, the mother is as new to the game as the baby. The adjustments can be mutually hazardous, particularly in the early months.

If I seem to put a good deal of emphasis on the term *mothering*, it is because of the key contribution we ascribe to it in terms of the baby's sound emotional development. *Mothering* means frequent physical contact with the baby. It means an infant snugly held. It means all the small physical details of caring for a baby, never performed in a perfunctory manner, but always in a way which makes the baby *feel* the parent's tender love. If we could ask the baby what he wants most from his mother, he would undoubtedly include frequent rocking, caressing, fondling, and the close sound of his mother's voice.

All of this may seem trivial to parents at a time when their baby seems little more than a vegetable. Many parents say to us, "After all, what kind of relationship is possible between me and this tiny thing that does nothing but sleep, wet, and wheeze occasionally?" The giving without expecting anything in return is precisely the substance of motherhood. All the love and attention showered on an infant in these crucial months will be returned a thousandfold in later years. Such a child will have a greater capacity to love and to give because of such a bountiful heritage from his infancy.

The best-meaning parents in the world, using

their own "scientific" theories of upbringing, will sometimes go contrary to their own instincts. Not too long ago, an eight-month-old child was referred to me. His parents were visibly worried. Each night he would violently rock himself back and forth in his crib to put himself to sleep. We soon discovered the cause: While the baby was physically well cared for, the mother has meticulously simulated in her own nursery all the antiseptic conditions of the hospital. The baby was always left alone to go to sleep. "Our nursery," she reported proudly, "is absolutely quiet and completely separated from the rest of the house." The father was not allowed to invade his child's sanctum for fear of unduly "exciting" the infant. Fortunately, the case was quite easily solved: After the mother had played with her child and rocked him to sleep for just a month, the habit stopped completely.

Can such mothering be overdone? Certainly not at this early state of life. Children are never spoiled or made over-dependent by generous affection in their infancy. If the mother's love is given regularly and expressed in normal ways, the child will always thrive in this environment of total emotional security.

The degree to which the mother gives of herself in this early relationship depends on her own emotional capacity and equipment. A woman's own childhood, her relationship particularly with her own mother, as well as with her husband, all determine her ability to cope with this entirely new relationship. We frequently note in therapy that mothers with a turbulent history in their own childhood find their own act of *mothering* difficult. They may prove excellent mothers in all other ways. But they miss something crucial when it comes to giving their infant a fully secure emotional environment. Barren childhoods rarely lead to excessively generous personalities in the later years.

Other problems, too, can easily impinge on a woman's basic ability to mother. Marital friction is a frequent example. Where a woman's own deeper emotional needs go wanting because of an unsatisfactory marriage, she is not very likely to give her very best to her child. The woman who receives the full emotional support of her husband is a far better equipped mother. A happy wife invariably makes a better mother.

What of the father's role during the baby's early months of life? Most fathers these days spend more hours commuting than they can possibly give to their babies. To all effects and purposes, the father must confine himself to a supporting role. Nonetheless, the effective father gives of himself unsparingly to his baby during whatever hours he is free to do so.

Adding a baby to the family—and especially the first one—can for the father be a very unsettling experience. Some fathers feel themselves neglected by their wife's primary attentions to the newborn child. Their complaint may be exaggerated; or they may suffer in silence. The fact remains that the new father finds himself competing with his child for his wife's attention and time. While he is not likely to express his feelings openly, he may harbor some dark thoughts about this tiny intruder.

Just as with his wife, his own childhood experiences may leave their mark on this new dilemma. The baby's constant demands on his wife's time may well recall his own childhood, when a new baby brother or sister seemed to replace him in the family constellation. It is worth repeating that no matter what the father's emotional difficulties may be, his ability to overcome them and support his wife at this crucial time will invariably reflect on their mutual success in parenthood.

Mothers are often surprised to learn that sound emotional development in the infant goes hand in hand with the child's physical progress. We see many cases each year, where placid appearance, underweight, and intestinal problems are the result of the child's having been denied basic emotional support in the early years.

Just how are the emotional and physical aspects of child development interlocked? Many parents I see cast a dubious eye at the proposition that a healthier baby is a result of anything more than the proper combination of milk, minerals, and vitamins. Perhaps this is because the emotional aspects of early growth are frequently slighted in baby care manuals.

Let us begin with breathing and sucking. These are among the most vital activities of the newborn child. Can these functions be stimulated by the emotional and physical support of the mother? The answer is, unquestionably, yes. Many babies experience difficulties in sucking vigorously enough to take in sufficient nourishment. In the first months of life, breathing tends to be shallow and irregular. More rapid and deeper sucking can be achieved through stimulating their mouths with the nipple, and holding the infant close to the mother's body. Proper breathing is essential to the development of the brain, which requires twice as much oxygen as other body tissues. Although oxygen is plentiful in the air, the baby's shallow breathing often minimizes the oxygen intake.

For the infant, breathing represents an entirely new experience. Before birth, his prenatal reliance on the mother's placenta made breathing unnecessary. But nature has provided beautifully here: A baby's first response to the mother's touch is respiratory. The more she fondles the baby, the more he will respond through deeper breathing.

No discussion of the first year of life would be complete without a few words about schedules. Feeding schedules today come in for a good deal of parental attention and concern. Precise feeding periods are the banners under which many embattled parents take their stand. However, many of us who work with children suspect that such parents may be picking the wrong issue at the wrong time. The newborn infant has not yet had an opportunity to consult the baby care manuals. He prefers to be fed when he is hungry and not by what the book may say. Regardless of what schedule he is on, the baby should always be fed when he is hungry. No attempt at discipline should be imposed. Serious emotional problems can arise if a baby has to endure constantly the discomfort and uncertainty of waiting for his bottle. Eating removes his pain, relieves tensions, and represents a pleasurable experience.

Poor feeding experiences at such an early age may result in lifelong emotional deprivations. Remember that whatever environment the infant finds himself in, his tiny world is the one he is most likely to adopt and carry on through much of his adult life.

Sudden changes in the intimacy of this routine in the early months can bring with it unforeseen consequences. I recall a warm and demonstrative mother, who, when her baby was five months old, was hospitalized after an automobile accident for an extended period. An elderly maiden aunt took over the baby's care. She was exceedingly conscientious, but at the same time totally incapable of meeting the child's emotional needs. All of the maternal attitudes were absent. The baby's skin began to show a marked pallor, indicating a regressing circulation. Intense thumb-sucking gave way to vomiting, diarrhea, insomnia, and perpetual restlessness. Fortunately, the mother was released from the hospital soon after the symptoms grew acute, and the baby soon resumed its normal development. Early recognition of the trouble is essential if we are to begin useful therapy. But if a child's basic needs continue to go unsatisfied, he will most likely do something to relieve himself of these deeply felt frustrations. Just what kind of frustration symptoms can we look for?

In the early stages of life, an infant's reaction is likely to take on one of three variations:

1. He will fight the cause.
2. He will run away from the cause.
3. He will become immobilized.

All three may be part of what is commonly called a pattern of "problem behavior." Functional feeding problems are common occurrences, even under the best of circumstances. An inadequate supply of breast milk, an incorrect chemical formula, a clogged or excessively free-flowing nipple can all conspire to make a baby's life miserable. A baby's reaction to his plight may vary: He may cry and kick, he may vomit, or he may turn away and refuse his bottle entirely.

Just how do such feeding difficulties relate to the baby's feelings toward his mother? He may blame his mother. He may automatically begin to turn away from her when she approaches, or he may cry in her presence. A few years later, he may refuse to do anything she suggests or do precisely the opposite.

Few problems engage more of our time in psychotherapy than those involving a child's abnormal feeding behavior. The problem may span the early beginnings of life to beyond adolescence. Causes are multiple, and parents are often surprised to learn how much long-term harm can be done by some undesirable experiences during the early months of life.

Children's feeding and eating behavior problems can often have been caused by some earlier parental misunderstanding. One of the most frequent stumbling blocks is the parents' routine. Most of us in clinical work are not anarchists, and the overthrow of proper feeding schedules is not among our most immediate objectives. But parents who worry unnecessarily about such things should acquaint themselves with certain important clinical studies conducted on a large number of infants. These studies show that exacting diets and feeding schedules are no assurance of a well-nourished child. In one famous study, fifteen children over a long period were served a large variety of foods, none particularly appetizing. No adult guidance was given as to what ought to be eaten. Some children were observed to gobble up several bananas in a row, while others found six or seven servings of potatoes more intriguing. No food was served between mealtimes. At the end of the experiment, none of the children was either overweight or underweight. All were in splendid health. The clinicians concluded that children over the long haul were perfectly capable of selecting their own well-balanced diets.

Eating problems are *least* likely to develop if mealtimes are a relaxed and pleasant part of the daily routine. If such fortuitous conditions prevail, few babies will develop worrisome symptoms, either in the early years or later on.

Making a big issue out of eating the right thing at the right time is an open invitation for a bout of willpower. Adults rarely win. We encounter innumerable situations where a child will use his eating periods as a means of controlling the situation around him. Eating behavior presents the child with a powerful weapon with which to retaliate or dominate an unsuspecting parent. It is part of our Western cultural heritage that we equate mother-love with finishing the plate. Nutritionally speaking, we might all live longer and better if we did *not* finish the plate.

"If you love Mommy, you'll finish your milk!" is an admonishment and a desperate challenge heard in a thousand households. But suppose the little one doesn't want to finish his milk this morning? The odds are in his favor, and he knows it. With unmerciful cunning, he knows that vomiting, or an utter refusal of all food, can throw an entire household into bedlam. The baby learns this soon enough, and he uses his new-found weapon well.

Eating problems that arise with her own children often have as their source a mother's own basic eating patterns. In those cases where a mother unconsciously rejects her child, she may tend to compensate (often quite unknowingly) for her guilt by overstuffing the child with almost morbid intensity. When we observe obesity in children, we often find a guilt-ridden mother.

I recall a mother coming to our clinic with two girls, aged eight and eleven. Both girls were immensely overweight. They were objects of ridicule, and had begun to show signs of emotional strain. After months of therapy with both mother and daughters, it emerged that the mother had wanted neither child. Both were "accidents," to use her own words. To compensate for her inner rejection of her children, she had spent years feeding them all possible quantities of food as the most demonstrable act of love she could think of. The children, in turn, reacted by eating all their mother demanded of them.

Abnormal eating behavior usually takes on one of two major forms in the early stages of life: Overeating, or a total refusal of food. Infants often show a general lack of interest in food over long periods, which in more serious cases extends to a loss of appetite, vomiting, and in extreme cases total refusal of food. As a last resort, such children sometimes require hospitalization as the only effective remedial treatment.

Children who habitually overeat do so for two primary reasons: they are either making up for a lack of satisfaction in their parent-child relationship, or they overeat in order to win parental approval. An emotionally starved child will frequently overemphasized his oral needs to such a degree that he lives in a continual drive for successive oral satisfactions. Overeating, then, is frequently a basic symptom of unhappiness, frustration, and lack of love, by the child as well as the adult.

Parents should make every effort to analyze the cause of feeding difficulties. First, an attempt should be made to pin down any emotional problems of their own. These have to do with their own childhood, and their very basic attitudes toward the child. If such analysis is not fruitful, outside counsel may be needed.

Secondly, the mother should make an all-out attempt to provide her child with an optimum feeding environment, and, irrespective of her own possible problems, eliminate the baby's frustrations so far as this is feasible. The mother who is more concerned and aware of her own relationship to her child, rather than with the food she wants him to have, is likely to find a happier solution.

In other ways as well she can help her baby form sound and normal feeding habits. It is always better to start with minimum helpings of food and have the child ask for more, rather than force into him an arbitrary amount. If the child doesn't finish his plate in fifteen minutes, it is better to remove the plate without comment or irritation.

To the infant, feeding and sucking are interchangeable. If the infant's sucking needs go unsatisfied, the demands for the bottle may extend far beyond the time such things are normally given up. What is "normal" for one baby may not be for another, but we consider three to four years the normal sucking period.

Most infants also require a minimum of two nonnutritive sucking hours each day. We are often amazed to see how many parents seriously attempt to thwart babies in this regard. Children who are allowed these extra periods of sucking will discontinue to suck as a normal sequence of development. However, parents who become upset about possible deformations of the mouth and stop the sucking by whatever means available may find their child's problems eventually go beyond that of orthodontia: food may be refused entirely, or the child may carry some permanent resentment toward one or both parents.

The world of the infant is a world of feeling. It is not yet a world of thought, or of analysis, or of reasoning about himself or the world about him. But no matter how immature the baby's over-all development, even the newborn baby is endowed with three well-developed sets of feelings. These are the sense of touch, the sense of body position, and the sense of sound.

The *sense of touch* is perhaps the most obvious one. It is most highly developed around the baby's mouth, from which most pleasure and satisfaction will be derived. Other areas, while not yet as sensitive to the touch, will soon develop as part of the baby's normal development. These are additionally sensitized by the mother's stimulation during bathing and dressing periods.

The baby's *sense of body position* is the second feeling. A firm but gentle hand, the rhythmic to and fro of a rocking chair, the close cuddling of parent and child: all contribute to his sense of security. It is a pity that so few modern nurseries are equipped with a cradle and a rocking chair. Their therapeutic value was much better appreciated by our grandmothers. The infant lives in a rhythmic world during his initial development in his mother's womb, and he misses this soothing movement in his modern nursery.

The baby's *sense of sound* develops early. Many of us have seen a baby start upon hearing some unexpected noise. Even the youngest of infants are extremely sensitive to unaccustomed sounds. This is not to say that infants thrive on a total vacuum of sound. They should soon enough be introduced to the routine sounds of family life. The sounds of toys, of splashing water, and soft voices are an excellent introduction to their ever-expanding world.

The mother's voice is most conducive to the emotional development of the child. I cannot over-emphasize its therapeutic effect on the baby's growing awareness of the outside world. Warmth of feeling is just as effectively conveyed through the mother's voice as it is through physical contact.

While this catering to a baby's needs may at times seem absurdly trivial to his parents, it is nonetheless true that so far as the feeling baby is concerned, they all satisfy his dominant need to be loved. The proof of the pudding lies in our frequent observation that where these parental stimuli are absent, infants often begin to act in disturbing ways. These may include head-rolling, head-banging, thumbsucking, and various other forms of hyperactivity or withdrawal in the early years. In later years, even more serious symptoms may arise, including speech disorders, eating problems, and gastric ulcers.

Many new parents seem worried about what they regard as the excessive sleeping habits of their baby. Babies in their very first stage of life really do not sleep in the adult sense. Instead, it is a continuation of their prenatal semi-conscious state. Up to about three months of age, normal babies can and will sleep twenty-two hours a day. After this stage, mental activity begins to quicken. Up to three months, however, fully conscious behavior over prolonged periods is rare. When does a baby's brain really begin to function? This is easy enough to discover. When he smiles, hearing his parents' voices, or when he reaches out for an object.

Developing relaxed and healthy sleep routines early in life strikes us as highly desirable. Mothers play an important role here. Without their mothers' help, babies will often resort to sucking as their only means of falling asleep. Rocking and singing to the baby still remain two of the best ways to accomplish this for him. They are old antidotes, but work as well in the jet age as they did in the horse and buggy days.

A baby should be kept close to his mother's side

during the first month of life, preferably in her bedroom. After that a separate but adjacent room is perfectly satisfactory. A sleep schedule of a minimum sixteen hours during the first two years of life is considered normal.

We should consider the emotional aspects of weaning. Some mothers, unfortunately, attach special social prestige to weaning their children at an extremely early age. They wear these triumphs as they once wore Girl Scout badges. Such attitudes are not only ludicrous; they can prove seriously harmful. I remember one mother who weaned her little boy at four months, and immediately thereafter left on a prolonged vacation. As she had breast-fed him, his deprivation was doubly meaningful, and she returned to a very unhappy and disturbed baby.

Forced weaning, like premature toilet-training, may represent a small social triumph but the basic logic escapes those of us who must eventually deal with its emotional consequences. Weaning ought not to be attempted before the ninth or tenth month of life. It should be a gradual transition, causing hardship neither on the child nor the parent. Semi-solid food should be introduced slowly and gradually in increasing portions. Bottle and cup ought to coexist peacefully for some time to come. If he is a normal child, the baby will most likely give up his bottle of his own accord.

Many mothers assume that once the weaning procedure is completed, all sucking should logically come to an end. Quite the contrary is true: in some children, the weaning from the bottle is often accompanied by an increase in non-nutritive sucking. This should cause no concern. Such sucking into the third and fourth year is quite normal, and provides a necessary satisfaction to the child.

Some parents resort to extremes in an attempt to cut out sucking. I recently consulted with a mother who weaned her child when he was five months old. The child compensated by sucking constantly, whereupon the mother tied his hands to his sides in a desperate effort to break his habit. Such measures are cruel and invite untold damage.

What can a baby think of such a mother? The human being he sees bending over his crib is his world. Through her he begins to respond and judge the human spirit. He now begins to form his own value judgments of likes and dislikes, not only for food but for people. If his mother is kind, considerate, soft, and sensitive, he will enter his world in justified expectations of a deeply felt life of his own. If she is hostile, impersonal, devoid of sentiment and warmth, she may prove one of the most unfortunate obstacles to a developing personality. It may lead him straight into the hard jungle of an impersonal existence and possibly a bitter adult struggle with his world.

We psychotherapists always think it a great pity that by the time we see these mothers with their troubled children, it is often a purely academic question whether or not the child's initial emotional experience was a positive one. Often he has already suffered emotional deprivation and irretrievable and serious harm has occurred.

Psychiatric therapists often lament the lost opportunities to forge a better balanced life for the emerging personality. Sometimes alert and intelligent parents read the warning signals in time. These are the fortunate ones, the wise ones: they are also the parents with the necessary inner security, so that seeking outside help poses no undue threat. They may then expect, hopefully, a satisfactory solution to the disturbances they suspect in their young.

The warning signals during the early period of life are often discernible. They usually take one of three forms. The baby may:

1. Develop anxiety symptoms.
2. Have feeding troubles.
3. Be antagonistic and negative.

Anxiety symptoms are often quite overt and are difficult to miss. They may occur in the form of frequent crying spells, difficulties in sleeping, or general restlessness.

Feeding problems may also become blatantly apparent. Feeding difficulties, as we have already seen, cover many varieties. Total refusal of food and rejection through vomiting are two of its most common forms.

Antagonistic children are commonly referred to by embattled mothers as "impossible children." These are the children whom parents say they "can't do anything with." Parents should remind themselves that the child may harbor similar reservations about *them*. What are now relatively small hurdles may grow into more serious and permanent forms of disorder in later life.

We must at all times deal with the *cause*, not the symptom. We assume such problems to have normally arisen out of one of these early childhood traumas:

1. The child has had a series of painful feeding experiences.
2. His need to suck for pleasure has been frustrated.
3. He has been frustrated in his search for mothering.
4. His need to grow in a tranquil and stable environment has been frustrated—either by a diffi-

cult marriage, difficult family circumstances, or other external disturbances.

A typical case will illustrate the point: Quite recently, Johnny R., seven years old, was referred because of serious speech and eating disorders. He not only talked with great difficulty, but for several years had refused almost all food except cold cereal. He sucked constantly, was a frequent bed-wetter and a slow learner in school, although he proved to be above average in intelligence.

After a series of interviews with both parents and Johnny's brothers and sisters, the sad picture emerged. Mr. R. was almost entirely removed from the family scene. He worked eighty to ninety hours a week, including most weekends. Johnny's mother, who had had a bad childhood of her own, was an unhappy and disillusioned wife. Johnny's own emotional history ran quite true to the same pattern: in his first year of life, he began to show breathing and feeding difficulties, followed by speech disorders.

Johnny had never received any of the basic emotional satisfactions which other children consider a matter of course. Mrs. R., totally overwhelmed by her own problems, could provide little emotional warmth. Her hostility to Mr. R. was unconsciously carried over to Johnny. With his own limited means, Johnny fought desperately to gain increased attention. He would not eat—an act of infantile defiance—and he would not talk. Alone in his crib, he sucked constantly and routinely for want of any other forms of gratification. As his symptoms increased, his mother became increasingly worried. Seven years later, she finally sought help. Unfortunately, a late decision.

There are many Johnnies. Many have what appear to be normal and intelligent parents. Nonetheless, many parents fail to give something of themselves in the early months and years of the child. In this case it was not forthcoming. Good common sense and a special kind of parental selflessness are two magic ingredients of success. Being aware of their essentiality is half the battle.

For the parent as well as the child, the first year of life is one of adjustment and transition. It is, above all, a time of giving. Parents will soon enough reap a rich bounty. Provide the child with all possible emotional gratifications now, and the child will grow into a living and enduring person. The lifelong dividends are incalculable.

IV

One to Three Years: The Ages of Discovery

No MATTER how many youngsters we observe in the course of our professional careers, few phases of life hold more fascination than the infant just emerging from his own small universe. One never tires of this marvelous spectacle, watching the two- or three-year-old seek and discover his own personality. Never are the parents' attitudes again to be quite so crucial to the child's development.

Whenever I discuss the child's various stages of development with a parent, I like to say that while the first year of life can best be characterized by the child's discovery of *"I AM!"* this next stage is simply, *"I AM ME!"*

In the first year of life, all babies may seem much alike. Take any hundred, average them out. You will find your share of tranquillity, tempers, diaper rashes, and sleepless nights. This comes as a shock to many a new parent—that his child is not yet an INDIVIDUAL. But now, individuality emerges in the second and third year of life. To develop fully into an individual is both a creative and abrasive process—meaning that the fine shaping and subtleties of human individuality are all a matter of repeated adjustments to the environment, and to the individuals around the child.

A child cannot become a person until he undergoes a wide series of tests and occasional crises.

These must be approached, faced, suffered through, tolerated. They run the whole wide gamut of the child's emotions. Just how well he adjusts to being a dues-paying member of humanity will largely depend on the parent.

In the preceding chapters, in which we described the first, the "oral phase," of life, we counseled parents to give and give again, even if it hurts. And it *does* hurt sometimes. No parent should be abashed at admitting that getting up three times at night after a harrowing day is not his or her ideal of parental bliss. Father is no less a parent for facing the fact that he is not exactly delighted with his nocturnal slavery. "But wait till the first year is up," he silently prays, "and he'll start fending for himself."

Let me say here and now that the giving does not stop—it merely changes dimensions. Let me put it more plainly: for those parents who confuse their child's developing self-expression and widening self-reliance as a parental passport to independence, the flag is already hoisted to half-mast! Giving to the one- and two-year-old takes on quite a different form of giving than before. Nonetheless, it is giving of a very special and vital kind.

You have to reduce certain words in your daily vocabulary, the most important of which is "NO!" There are many others. To give a full list would be impossible, but do these sound familiar? "Don't touch!" "You mustn't!" "Stop playing with the glass!" or "Can't you leave anything alone?" Add all these up and string them next to each other, and it becomes one dreary nagging dialogue. That is precisely how it sounds to the child.

"Patience has its limits," you may say, and so it has. But a parent's patience becomes far more elastic once some understanding exists of just what the stakes are in the developing child's search for individuality. Some insights may come from a reading of this chapter. I think you will see why it becomes important to put some controls on your normal adult frustrations at seeing an enveloping crumbling world of disorder and chaos in your living room or kitchen. A good sense of humor helps, and a reverse time machine to take you back to your own childhood! We should try to understand this phase from our child's viewpoint. We must have a reasonably accurate idea of *what* our child is capable of and *when,* placed in terms of his individual development.

All of which may seem to be sheer anarchy. No one, of course, is suggesting that the two-year-old is licensed to domineer over the entire house. All I suggest is a healthy balance of providing sufficient play for the child's groping for his own self-being, and the necessary setting up of fences beyond which he cannot go. Before we discuss the finer points of a well-balanced parent-child relationship and the code of conduct that goes with it, a few words should be said about the parents' own emotional makeup. You may want to be the very best mother on your block, but there may be some deep-seated reasons why even your best efforts may prevent you. The very behavior of your child can ignite certain emotional reactions of your own which you may find hard to control. Emotional armors are easily pierced. No parent should think that his maturity is his impenetrable shield. Our clinics are full of families in which the parent was absolutely sure of his own righteousness.

While all of us have some emotional quirks, identifying particular ones can only come from individual self-analysis and therapy. In all cases, your own self-understanding will affect your emotional relationship with your child.

Very often, difficulties arise because of the gaps between the mother's actual emotions and her idea of how she "ought" to feel. Have you felt, for example, that mothers *always* love their children, and children *always* love their mothers? Let us see what happens on a day when you feel annoyed and irritated by your child's behavior. All of which, I might add, you are probably perfectly justified in feeling. What happens? For one thing, you may ravel yourself into a tight little knot of nerves. Then come Anxiety and Guilt! Not two very comfortable companions to have around, when you are supposed to love your child always. Pretty soon your anxiety turns to self-accusation. You begin to have doubts about your ability as a good mother. Sometimes, you go even further. You say to yourself that you didn't deserve to be a mother in the first place; you may even regret marriage, womanhood, your very existence. By then you are in a pretty fix, and your self-doubts keep gnawing away.

This may be carrying a situation to extremes, but we all know to what extent emotions can control our lives. Anxiety enters because you are taking issue with yourself as to whether or not you are a good parent. The fact of the matter is that all of these emotional upsets are part and parcel of being human. Let's face up to the fact that it is perfectly natural to get angry and even to entertain a hint of hostility along with feelings of love for your child.

Such strident feelings separate human mortals from the gods. When we can quite comfortably accept the fact that we can accommodate love and hate without acute emotional indigestion, we have already taken a big step forward. These feelings are, after all, part of all relationships in life. When we accept this hostility in ourselves, how much easier it becomes to deal with identical emotions in our children! These, too, will come, as surely as an upset stomach or a bruised finger.

Your child will soon enough develop ambivalent feelings of his own. He will love you and hate you. These will come in gushes, uncontrolled. Contrary to adult emotions, however, your child's hostility will be quite primitive, raw, and direct, and will be far more difficult to control than your own. That is why we often refer to sudden outbursts of temper in adults as "childish" or "infantile." In adults, these outbursts are a sign of failure in their life adjustment. In the child, they are perfectly normal and we should accept them as a child's way of flexing his emotional muscles.

Much of your child's entire future personality depends on the regard he will have for himself as well as for you and other human beings. The stakes are high and worth considerable effort. During this stage you as the parent represent a giant mirror in which he can see himself. Will you be a true mirror, in which he can see himself, or one of those distortion mirrors at the amusement park? This is difficult to answer, but we find that many parents who think of themselves as being accurate reflectors of their children are really not.

In grasping for his individuality, the child begins to say, "I AM ME." He can learn about himself only through you. He conjures up an image of himself through your own impression of him. He is, in short, as you see him. If you have confidence and trust in his ability to grow and learn, he *will* grow and learn. One of the basic principles of physics is the law that for every action there is a reaction. A similar law applies to our emotional makeup. It is just as basic: no human being can begin to love until he has first been loved. No human being can have self-respect until he is first respected himself.

So far we have discussed two requisites for the development of your child. The first is your own knowledge of what to expect of his groping toward individuality. The second has to do with your accepting your own feelings of ambivalence—of love and hate—so that you can better accept his own similar feelings.

And so, forearmed and forewarned, we approach the emotional growth of the two-year-old. He has now graduated into a new phase of life. This second year is full of adventure. We call this adventure the "anal" or toilet-training phase. It lasts longer than the first year's "oral" phase, and in many ways represents far more of a challenge to the parent. In fact, the road of the two-year-old can be long and occasionally tortuous—very much like Dorothy's in the *Wizard of Oz*. But like the story it all comes out well in the end, if you are willing, prepared, and, above all, patient.

I have already implied how extraordinarily important this second phase is. Not only does the child's life change radically within a span of two to three years, but the parent's attitudes toward the child change equally. During the first year of life, parents tend to keep their children overdependent. Babies are cuddled and cooed over, recommended therapy for the parent as well as for the baby.

But now comes the second stage. And who would ever have thought that the youngsters are the only ones to be weaned? The average parent throws a protective cocoon over the infant long after the need for it has disappeared. Some parents are reluctant to let their little ones experience things themselves. And how we can sympathize! There is nothing like a swaddling infant. It is a period of great magic in any happy marriage. Such moments do not repeat themselves, or at least not very often.

It is hard for some of us to realize that life moves at an amazingly rapid pace, especially if you are a one-year-old. Grown-ups often try to hold back the passing of time. They hesitate to let their babies feed themselves. They are often overprotective when the one-year-old ventures new skills.

On the other hand, there are those who, as if by the clock, want to push their one-year-olds out into the world, as if their youngsters had suddenly grown up at the stroke of midnight. True, there are certain milestones, like drinking from a cup, but they are merely stepping stones to something else.

Let us take a look at the weaning process. What a Waterloo this can be, a real frustration for your child. We are now depriving him of his primary satisfaction, that sucking. Sucking offers pleasures to the child which go far beyond those of the experience of eating. To him, sucking has been a fundamental and quite necessary form of gratification. Now he is being asked to surrender something that has been utterly basic all his life! And who is taking it away from him? MOTHER! His own mother, upon whom he has so totally depended for his life security. She now removes one of his basic security symbols. I may be forgiven for dramatizing this important milestone in a very young life, but it *is* a milestone, which parents should well recognize. Just because they have drunk from a cup for so many years should not make them feel so superior, nor so complacent, to the plight of their child. May *their* own parents have been as understanding!

It is never a question then of whether a child should be weaned, but *how* he should be weaned. Parents who handle this transition with patience and sensitivity find no particular difficulty or latent complications. The weaning process can be smooth and accomplished with no ill effects. But if the baby is forced to give up the bottle too soon or too quickly, problems may very well crop up. Breaking such a basic habit is particularly difficult for an infant, who cannot develop any alternate satisfactions.

Just what happens when children are abruptly "broken" from the bottle habit? They often become tense and anxious, a state of mind which shows in many ways. Often, they will display their anxiety by refusing food entirely. Some children choose to be more diabolic: they will agree to take the food, only to vomit it forth in abrupt profusion. Should their astonished parents regard this as a visible sign of hostility, they would be absolutely right. It is written in a language which a child can express most eloquently.

If your child chooses not to take this route, he may exhibit hyperactivity and tension during the day and restlessness during the night. Far too many mothers have proudly shown off their two- or three-year-olds as being "so full of life," that they simply don't know what to do with them. If they could only have realized that their pride might too often turn into anguish in later years! Weaning, like toilet-training, should not be used as a prop for a parent's ego. The world is full of such parents who place the overnight weaning of their eight-month-old alongside other family trophies such as a second car in the garage and a crabgrass-free front lawn. While the alternatives to a perfect lawn are crabgrass and chickweed, the consequences of forceful and premature weaning or toilet-training are much more serious.

Just when the "right" time arrives for complete weaning depends on the individual child. We often like to assure the worried parent that a child who is weaned at eighteen months has as much opportunity to become president of the United States as a child weaned at ten months. He may also be a happier and more effective president. There is absolutely no virtue in being weaned earlier or later, except as it affects the emotional needs of the parent. But this is really not the point. Let us say that the average age at which a child will wean himself comes around the end of the first year. Most mothers find that the process can be considerably eased by gradually introducing the cup without withdrawing the bottle entirely.

What about toilet-training? More of the parents' own attitudes and sense of balance are involved in toilet-training than almost any other problem. The precise reason why it is so emotionally charged for some adults is of at least equal interest to sociologists and anthropologists as for those of us who deal with the day-to-day adjustments of growing up. Suffice it to say that toilet-training easily conjures up conflicts, and we must look into the matter in some depth before hoping to cope with it successfully.

For the child, the process of excretion is one of the most pleasurable moments of his daily routine. He knows nothing yet about our society's enchantment with antiseptic bathrooms and the adult's need to disguise the bathroom function for anything but what it really is. It is, after all, never the toilet, but the bathroom, the "John," or the powder room. For the child, it is against all of his basic instincts to master control over his elimination. In fact, it is physically impossible for him, if toilet-training is thrust upon him too early in life.

The typical small child would like nothing better than to smear his stool all over the wall. To his mother, this may very well be a "disgusting" performance. But he does not understand the shock of his parents and the distaste with which they may regard his behavior. Many parents have feelings left over from their own childhood, and they find it difficult to accept the primitive impulses in their youngsters. Only let us remember that the sense of shame is the parent's, not the child's.

Those of us who are professionally close to the problems cannot help but take a bird's-eye view of our contemporary social setting: how often, I am afraid, does an unusually early toilet-trained child become the pride of the preening mother? Gladys arrives in triumph at her Wednesday Afternoon Bridge Club and proclaims to the sound of faraway trumpets that Walter is now toilet-trained at the fantastic age of nine and a half months, when Irma's little daughter next door didn't quite make it at ten months! However, she neglects to tell the girls that that same morning she has taken her prodigal son to her pediatrician to see why her little darling throws back his cereal at her. But there it is. Society has been served. Gladys has had her moment of glory.

Seriously, and speaking from a broad experience, there is ample evidence that premature and excessively forced toilet-training *can* leave traumatic bruises, which are not often overcome even much later in life. This pressure of some parents to toilet-train their youngsters as early as possible, and accomplish it as quickly as possible, can be devastating to the child's development and emerging personality.

A child is neurologically rarely ready to be trained before his second year. If the mother succeeds in having her little one on the toilet seat at the time he is ready to eliminate, this is most often a matter of sheer luck and accident, and a credit of course to the parent's perserverance and sense of timing. But that is all. It is no more than that!

Pressures at early training often leave the child with all kinds of frustrations, some of them not easily erasable. Psychologically as well as physically, the child is far better prepared to make the transition toward the latter part of his second year. By then, the child takes a natural interest in that part of his body, and his entry into the anal period makes this a natural focus of his concentration. Attempting to toilet-train him at a time when he still seeks primarily oral satisfactions is really putting the cart before the horse.

Some of the more unfortunate consequences of premature training are not too readily visible. The child that is pressured and pushed into doing something that is not yet possible or easily attainable can quickly grow into an insecure child. He feels that the other people in his home are not considering *his* needs. Rather than follow the dictates of his body, he is asked to follow a routine imposed from the outside. Rather than learning to control his body, he moves further away from it: he becomes less sure of himself, less sure of his parents' love and understanding. Even if he appears to comply with his parents' insistence on changing his toilet habits, his anxiety grows, and his anger at them and at his own difficult situation often mushrooms into something bigger.

Frequently, these youngsters will not show their anger directly. They are afraid to lose their parents' love. They become a behavior problem instead: a problem of temper tantrums, of bullying other children, of being destructive to objects as well as violent in their own fantasies. On the surface, toilet-training may have been accomplished, but certain baffling behavior problems may soon crop up as symptoms of basic frustrations.

Other youngsters may not give in that easily. Suppose your youngster has the kind of makeup which makes him decide to fight it out. His bowel movements after all are his own. You cannot force them out if he chooses not to give them to you. If he decides upon a cold war, things can become rather interesting, but extremely frustrating for both sides. The more you push him, the more he will resist. He will soil and wet after he is taken off his toilet seat. Or he may not even be as generous and may decide to stop functioning altogether.

But it need not be so. This kind of situation need not develop in the first place. Patient handling of the toilet-training function will provide the child with wonderful opportunities of showing cooperation, good will, and willingness to conform. Are these not qualities which we all expect to see in each other later in life? You will not only help your child to master elimination, but you will establish for him the desirability of adjusting to life by what we call the "reality principle." It means that, as time goes on, your child will be able to sublimate his own gratifications, when he faces demands for conformity at school, at his job, his community, or in his own home. Who does not know youngsters who are unable to adjust to school and social functions, of adolescents who live

outside the community's normal code of behavior,
or of older people who have never adjusted to authority in their own work?

Toilet-training at the right time and in the right
way carries profound rewards. Those children who
during this period find it hard to give of themselves feel usually that they have been taken advantage of, that they are being used, bullied, and
pushed around. In this case as many others, the
parents' own example is the best teacher. If these
early years have been characterized by tolerance,
devotion, and understanding of the child, he will
begin to identify with the parent. He will most
likely want to be the same kind of person his own
parent is. He will want to be and do exactly what
he sees in others whom he loves and respects. But
there is little incentive for him to emulate, if this
love and respect is not apparent to him.

I think it needs emphasizing that even under the
best circumstances, the best adjusted child may
pass through some stormy moments. This is quite
normal and should neither discourage nor alarm.
Even the normal child goes through some fairly
radical changes in these very early years, and the
degree to which he can pass through this period
with comparative equanimity is as much up to the
parent as it is to the developing child. Now, for
the first time, he will and must begin to give of
himself. Whereas he was allowed up to now to be
totally irresponsible, he must now respond to outside pressures and *be* responsible. Very soon, the
process of conforming to certain standards of behavior, as imposed by his elders, descends upon
him in various ways. Not only must he *not* kick
the furniture, *not* break the china, and *not* put
crayon on the wallpaper, but he must actively begin to show some success in his own cleanliness, to

put his toys where they ought to be, to learn the basic forms of politeness, and—hopefully—to learn to share his possessions with others.

Conformity is closing in all around him. The normal child is not overly disturbed by this, so long as he knows that for every act of conformity he will also receive love and respect for his own emerging personality.

What the child must now face up to represents entirely new challenges. Will he rebel or capitulate? If he rebels and refuses, he must contend with his parents' disapproval. A young child that faces disapproval is also a much-chagrined child. He is totally dependent on his parents' love and approval. If this is denied him, deep anxiety is often a result. Anger follows anxiety, created by his own inability to cope with his parents' disapproval. Hostility toward his parents is the inevitable result since it is they who have put him in such an untenable position.

But let us look at the child's hostility: this hostility is pure, simple, and primitive. It is *not* hostility as we adults know it. With us, hostility is normally the result of maladjustments to an environment. For us parents, hostility, normally only transitory, does not blind us to such inner emotions as respect, tolerance, and even love. We can be angry with our loved ones, knowing all the time that the love of many years will not falter for these angry moments. But the child is different. With him it is all white or all black: he cannot love and be angry at the same time. We must be aware that our child feels either pure anger or pure love. The child assumes that his elders' emotions function the same as his, that his father's or mother's anger means that their love has been totally withdrawn, and that he faces a permanently hostile environment. To the young child, a parent's disapproval, a reprimand, and even routine discipline may seem to express total hostility.

This situation of course should not obviate the parents' need to carry on their obligations as parents and teachers. Discipline is necessary, so long as it is just. And soon, by gradual and repeated experiences, the child begins to learn that both hate and love *can* coexist at the same time.

The mother who herself has solved her own ambivalent feelings toward her parents, or her husband and friends, will be fully equipped to handle her own child's ambivalence. Normal adjustments in the parent breed normal life adjustments in the child. Ambivalence, we must remember, in our own feelings is a part of living. We handle it without guilt, without distortion or repressions. Let your child know that anger and love are both the same ball of wax. It is perfectly normal to feel the way he does. Let him know it, and he will learn how to handle his hostility and ride out his little storms without capsizing.

Once the child understands that hostility can live side by side with love and security, the rough edges of adjusting himself to this widening world of his gradually disappear. Eventually, these conflicts of his—shall be submit to keep his parents' love, or shall he rebel and express his anger?—will take on entirely different tones.

The child learns soon enough that his own outbursts of anger may come and go, but his elders' love is constant. Quite soon, his parents' "no's" become easier to accept. He finds it easier to acquiesce to his parents' wishes. Sooner or later, he will whisper "no" to himself—the beginnings of a budding superego! Watch a two- or three-year-old eye that gleaming piece of crystal on the shelf above him, and he will say "no" to himself.

To the two- and three-year-old, the horizons of his world now begin to widen perceptibly. Too many parents, I am afraid, want to push open the doors to this new world before the child is physically or emotionally prepared. Premature efforts are often taken to force talking, cleanliness, and cooperation.

What about speaking? Old wives' tales die hard, but an early talker does not make an Einstein. At least, one does not necessarily follow the other. Coercion will not cause your child to talk one day earlier. Keep in mind that any small single human being who is trying to make monumental strides in such diverse areas as toilet-training, walking, and talking really has quite a lot to handle. Not all progress will come equally, or at the same time. It will be halting—a walk here, a talk there. You can help his speaking best by giving him your attention, your interest, and especially your conversation. You can prove to him that by talking to him, you and he can arrive at a closer and more harmonious relationship.

But growing up brings problems along with independence. He will bang himself against the chair, he will fall during his first and often futile attempts to walk he may soil his underwear and cause himself discomfort. All these trials and errors may lead to more frequent crying, which may not worry him half as much as it does you. If you have given him enough love and attention in the course of all these months, he is not apt to cry as a purely attention-seeking device. More likely, he will cry when he is genuinely hurt or uncomfortable, when he really needs your comfort and consoling.

If cleanliness is next to godliness, the good

Lord must worry especially about some of His youngsters. Cleanliness can be a source of many problems. I can best illustrate this by citing a four-year-old boy, Edward. Edward's nursery teacher referred him because of his inordinate fear of getting dirty. Now this, you might say, was never the problem of *your* youngster. But Edward's fear to dirt was so exaggerated that he would panic at the sight of his own soiled clothing or soiled hands. He tried to avoid getting dirty by withdrawing from all activities. Sitting idly by without doing anything seemed to him the safest solution. It was strange behavior, but a look into his family history soon gave us some interesting clues.

Interviews with his mother revealed her to have distorted views about cleanliness. A compulsive housekeeper, she spent her days cleaning the house to the exclusion of giving any attention whatever to her son. Things were carried so far as to force the boy to remove his shoes upon entering the house. The mother equated dirt with sinfulness. To young Edward, being dirty not only meant being bad, but also not being loved.

I only cite this case as an example of the results of extreme parental behavior—even on the subject of cleanliness! Particularly at this age, to have fun may indeed mean playing with mud and water, with clay and fingerpaints. The wise mother will view all these things in balance: let him know it is all right to play with dirt; that it can be washed off when the play period is over, and provide him with appropriate facilities.

While trying to keep a youngster clean is a point of considerable frustration to many parents, the matter of obeying the parents' orders and requests creates at least as many upsets for the child. We might as well face up to the fact that obedience is not the dominant virtue of the two- or three-year-old! He feels the exaggerated need of proving himself, to assert himself for the first time as an independent individual. Thus conflict with those around him becomes almost inevitable. How can he be an individual? Well, to the child, the easiest claim to independence is to say "No." It sounds good to him, and is bound to get a rise out of his parents. It rarely fails. Try to counter his "no's" with moderation, and react only when necessary.

Much of the secret to your own success in making your requests understood and complied with is the manner in which you ask your child to obey your direction. Friendliness combined with firmness is usually the prudent combination. Threats rarely work, and only bring forth further cascades of "no's." Offer threats and alternatives only when you really mean them and can follow through. Remember that your child will pay more attention to five reasonable rules than to fifteen inessential ones! Such are the simple mathematics of the three-year-old!

Perplexed parents often wonder how to handle a child's periods of negativism. Such periods can only be prolonged if the parent behaves as obdurately as the child. Tact and consideration in handling a child at this age will sooner than not obviate his need to fight you on every possible issue. Give him sufficient lead to assert his own will and exercise his independence where it does not conflict with others, and the child will not be pressured. On the contrary, he will live in an environment where his emotional needs are being satisfied in well-balanced proportions.

Parents often ask whether or not they should allow their children to hit them or other children in anger. The answer is "No." All children express violence at times, but there are important distinctions as to the cause of the violence. Parents should never let their children hit them as an expression of their anger. Rather, parents should attempt early to help the child verbalize his anger, to talk it out. This is not to say that his anger should go unnoticed: on the contrary, such feelings are best recognized and discussed. To say to a child, "You are very angry with Mommy because she won't let you twist the dog's tail," is very meaningful to the child. "It's all right to be angry. Mommy understands, but you cannot hit Mommy, and you cannot twist the dog's tail. You can talk about it or go and hit your Mommy dolls, but you cannot hit Mommy."

You should keep in mind the same goal in helping channel your child's hostility toward other children. He should not hit, kick, or bite other youngsters, no matter what age, except in self-defense. When a child has mastered his own anger and gets it out by talking about it, he will have achieved a far more relaxing relationship with the world around him. The child who is constantly at the mercy of his own impulses and attacks at the slightest provocation will make a poorly adjusted adult as well.

Your own behavior as a parent plays just as important a part here. If you yourself strike your child in anger, he will be prompted to do likewise, no matter how nicely you may rationalize and attempt to train him otherwise. The philosophy of "Don't do as I do, but do as I say" has very little appeal for children. In the field of anger and hostility, as well as so many others, your child will be what you are yourself!

V

The Oedipal Period: The Maturing Child

PARENTS REACT to the Oedipal stage, from three to six, in many interesting ways. It is one thing to see the stark human drama of Hamlet come full circle on stage, but quite another to have it reenacted in one's own living room.

To a few parents at least, their child's Oedipal stage seems to produce acute embarrassment. This parental awkwardness I long ago accepted with my mind, but never quite with my heart. As it usually happens, the "Hamlet in the Living Room" act follows a fairly traditional scenario: the four-year-old discovers sex. The romance may fail or reasonably succeed, depending on the understanding and capacity of the parent. The limitations of this Oedipal courting soon become obvious to most children. He recognizes he cannot have everything he wants, and the parent's tact will have much to do with his acceptance of reality.

We are now discussing the period of the "Triangle." Every family with a child three to seven years old suffers through it, and all normal families survive. It is laden with pathos and humor, and spattered with bursts of infantile romancing and occasional parental frowns. This is the time of the family romance, when every self-respecting little girl falls in love with her father, and every red-blooded little boy falls in love with his mother.

In some families, such romances are carried on under the very noses of their parents without either being particularly aware of them. "I want to marry Daddy" is a wish little girls often express openly. The mother, in this case, is not the third party in the triangle. It never becomes quite clear to either parents or these lovesick youngsters how they could "dispose" of their adult rival, nor is it ever seriously considered. Parents can rest assured that their youngsters mean them no harm, even though one of the two happens to be "in the way."

I have approached this Oedipal period somewhat lightly because it conjures forth all kinds of dread and threatening fears in some parents. Some think their youngster's Oedipal behavior "indecent." I know a few parents who seemed quite ready for the confessional chamber, thinking, I suppose, of the forbidding sins of incest. When I tell them that all of these things are a natural part of growing up, they look at me in stark disbelief.

There are other parents who treat this entire episode with purposeful ridicule, or a certain naive indifference. "Quit being a mommy's boy" is a much repeated phrase of an unnerved father who doesn't want his son "hanging around Mother" all the time. The truth, of course, is that the father has nothing to fear. His overt rejection of his little boy speaks for a father who shows a good deal of insensitivity to his son as a human being.

Unfortunately perhaps, few of us can remember the period in our own lives when we went through precisely the same kind of romance. If we were to recall it accurately, we would be struck by the close cause-and-effect relationship between the success of our own Oedipal romance and our own marriage later on. No man has ever happily and success-fully loved a woman without having loved his mother first. Nor has any woman made an entirely successful marriage partner without having loved and cherished her own father at one time or another.

To sum up, love of a parent is a pretty serious affair in the eyes of a four- or five-year-old. Parents should respect it for what it is.

The young boy wants to marry his mother, to take care of her, sleep with her, and if possible, keep Father at a safe distance. So, too, with the little girl: she will seek out a similarly close relationship with her father, and hope to replace her own mother. Just how we resolve the conflicts and some of the possible problems which can arise during this phase has a vital bearing on our children's later lives, on their relationships to others, and especially on the outcome of their own marriages.

Invariably, as I have already pointed out, this is a romance in which the little boy or girl loses out. Perhaps, this is the very reason why we adults rarely recall with any degree of accuracy our own Oedipal experiences. Most of us look back on youth and regard that part of our lives as strings upon strings of carefree days, weeks, and years. Actually, childhood is frequently blotched by heartache, frustration, and disappointment. Once we recognize this fact of a child's life, we can more readily provide the love, the patience, and the understanding which our children will need—particularly during their Oedipal period.

Contrary to the beliefs of some people, let me assure parents that the child's especially natural attraction to one of the parents is entirely natural and inevitable. It has little to do with the attitudes and behavior of the parents themselves. Most well-adjusted mothers want their little girls to love their fathers, and fathers want their boys to love their mothers. But having said that, subtle differences of approach and handling can color the entire parent-child relationship. Once a father, for example, recognizes the dynamics that apply, he will find it just as easy to say to his son upon leaving for the office, "Take care of Mommy now," instead of, "Now you do what your mother tells you to do!" The first implies a make-believe partnership as a junior father, the other denies this possibility entirely.

All of this Oedipal romancing serves a highly useful psychic purpose. It is a part of the process of growing into a more mature human being. Frequently, this trying-out period represents a very first attempt at a bisexual relationship. It is accompanied by acts of rebellion, jealousy, and hostility, all part of the growing-up process. These rebellions will happen irrespective of the parents' attitude toward these family dynamics.

Your child's sexual life, in its broad sense, actually begins some time before the onset of the Oedipal stage. During the first period of existence the pleasures of eating are pretty well developed. His thumb-sucking actually becomes one of his first sexual pleasures. It is one of the first pleasures to be discovered which he derives from his own body. We regard both the anal and oral phases as *sexual* phases, since both phases are characterized by physical pleasures of distinct kinds.

Once a child reaches three or thereabouts, his discovery of the sensual pleasures takes him to fondling his reproductive organs. Clinicians refer to this next phase as the *phallic* or Oedipal stage. In his stage the child experiences private sexual pleasures through masturbation and various fantasies normally associated with such activities. It is not until after puberty that the near-adult enters into the *genital* stage in which fully gratifying sex experiences and relations with the opposite sex can become possible. In the intervening years, particularly during the latency years, sexual drives are usually repressed.

During the previous stage, we will remember, just how your child related to you *as an individual* became a significant guidepost. You reflected the world to the young toddler, and it was important that the mirror held up to him was as undistorted as we know how to make it.

In the *Oedipal* phase, the spectrum of the child's most immediate interest widens to focus on both parents in married partnership. It furthermore involves the question as to how you as a couple relate to him as the focus of your dual attentions. To happily married couples, this period of a youngster's life rarely represents a problem. But any clinic's files are full of cases where unsuccessful marriages have affected the youngster's development particularly negatively during this Oedipal period. To put it more directly, your own success as a married man or a married woman becomes of utmost importance at this time.

It is inevitable that we should discuss the matter of sex education. Had this book been written a generation ago, eyebrows would have been raised at any hint of sex education of a child who was not a teen-ager. But in the 1960s, we have generally recognized that questions about sex should be responded to when they are asked. They ought never to be swept under the carpet and rejected. Sex happens to be a prime concern during the Oedipal period. It is therefore the best time to handle such questions with as much directness and with as little embarrassment as possible.

What you are willing to tell your child about sex will in large measure depend upon your own attitudes on the subject. Since this is a book about children and not about parents, we can only accept the parental sex attitudes that already exist and hope that they will suitably equip the parent to respond to the child's questions.

It is invariably best to present the facts of life *now*, at the Oedipal stage, rather than wait until he or she is twelve or thirteen. To those parents who might shudder at the thought and hesitate, it might help to remind them that children's sex interests are far more innocent than most adults'. Any fears we might have of "dirtying" their minds are based on our own attitudes. They are not founded on those of the six- or eight-year-old. Here, at this age, we set the roots for all knowledge. But silence only encourages the forbidding mysteries about sex which are bound to be all the more intriguing later on in life if information is now suppressed. Furthermore, it isn't always just *what* we tell our youngsters but *how* we convey what we want them to know. Whether your child will regard sex as "dirty" and "sinful" rather than natural and beautiful is pretty much up to you, the parent.

We will understand this natural curiosity about sex a bit better once we can gain a little foresight and see just what goes on in a child's mind. We know from clinical observation that around the age of three, the young boy's love for his mother changes in character. It slowly changes from the typical baby's dependent and narcissistic relationship to his mother to one in which he begins to recognize, if unconsciously, that his love for his mother is becoming something on the order of the way "Daddy loves Mommy."

Naturally, conflicts then arise: suddenly, the father, whom the boy also loves, becomes his rival; in fact, a strong rival with power to punish and control this very junior aspirant. With what is frequently rather vague inner logic, the boy seeks some way to get rid of his father. What is worse, he may very well fear that his resentment will be discovered by his father, and that his father will somehow retaliate.

The latter can be very frightening to a boy, and it is worth going into some detail. If the boy during his Oedipal period is frightened of possible paternal reprisals, he may very well fear for his genital organs, since he may become convinced that his father is out to destroy his masculinity. This fear is commonly referred to as the "castration complex." For the same reason, it is never wise for parents to jest with a little boy of this age about "cutting it off." Similarly, siblings and other family members should be discouraged from references of this kind.

This fear of father's "counterattack" also suppresses the normal boy's hostility toward his father, as well as the sexual feelings toward his mother. Nonetheless, his yearnings for his mother still subsist, and he may be for a time desperately unhappy and often resentful. After all, she will not accept the kind of love *he* wants to give. Nor will she accept him as an adult, but as a child.

It is quite easy to see how feelings of inadequacy can arise out of the twin prospect of a mother's nonacceptance of the boy's love and the father's uncontested superiority. Sometimes, a boy will compensate for such feelings of inadequacy by becoming an exhibitionist, to convince himself and others that his genital organs are safe and intact. Such behavior at this stage is of a quite different order than when carried on by an adult.

There is a corollary here, incidentally, that is worth noting: in the process of competing successfully with his father, the typical boy will try to become like his father, in order to be more loved, he feels, by his mother. In other words, he tends to identify more strongly, and to imitate his father in values and attitudes. His sense of morals as well as his superego begin to form.

During the latter part of the Oedipal period we increasingly see youngsters competing successfully with others of their own age groups. Their drives to compete increase as time goes on, as does their need to prove themselves. A boy's curiosity about sex gradually broadens to curiosity about knowledge generally.

Parents with young daughters know only too well that their entry into the Oedipal period tends to be somewhat more complex. Girls, after all, must switch their primary affection from the mother to the father in the fourth and fifth years of their lives. For the girl, the Oedipal period can create a great deal of anxiety. Instinctively, she will turn to her mother in time of need, to find the security of the dependency relationship which she has relied on since she was born. The greater the anxiety of the moment, the greater of course the need to hold on to what amounts to an infantile protective relationship.

We can see easily the potentials for conflict: as she grows, the girl must surrender much of what she feels she instinctively requires. She now turns to her father as a love object. Usually the young girl also makes the early discovery that, in one important sense, she will never mean quite as much to her father as her mother, and that it is folly to compete with her on that basis. As soon as this happens, some form of rivalry with her mother naturally occurs.

With girls as well as boys, sex education is a far easier matter to handle at this inquiring age. The other day I happened to eavesdrop on a conversation of two seven-year-olds, my own little girl and a boy. In discussing whether a rabbit they had just found was a boy or a girl rabbit, my little girl advised: "Turn it upside down and let's see if it has a penis." "What's a penis?" he asked. My little daughter didn't hesitate for a moment. "That's what boys have and girls don't," she told a wide-eyed boy, "but anyway, girls can have babies, and boys can't." This, one surmises, is a preview of the battle of the sexes, as played in one family's backyard.

A girl's emotions will rebound between her desire to be a boy and an inner feeling that she should recognize what she really is. If a girl is lucky enough to have a mother who feels secure as a woman, who is happy in her marriage, these potential conflicts usually resolve themselves. A girl's thinking will often go something like this: Since Mother seems very happy and shows no desire to be a man, and finds pleasure in the company of a man, perhaps I, too, should accept my role as a woman.

If, however, the mothers themselves have distorted views on the subject, it is easy to imagine the problems which can arise vis-a-vis an impressionable daughter.

Have you ever thought how *you* would act if you were to fall in love with your best friend's husband? It would be a terrible dilemma. Now think of your little girl, who faces a similar triangle. You are her best friend. You also happen to be married to the man she herself is in love with!

The healthy youngster resolves these conflicts with three basic mechanisms: Repression, Sublimation, and Identification. Repression is the most frequent form of resolution. By repression, the child blots out of his conscious world what he cannot have or cannot endure. This might include his desire for his mother, as we have already seen. Repression also forces into the unconscious guilt and anxiety feelings which are difficult to accept or bear. These can include the intense feelings of jealousy and hostility which a boy may feel for his father. Repressing such feelings relieves him of tensions. He can then relate to his parents without such conflict.

Some children resolve their conflicts by redirecting through sublimation or displacement. In this way, they can work off their inner drives which are unacceptable to their ego. Or they can redirect them toward other people as well as other activities.

The process of identification plays one of the most important functions during the Oedipal period. It creates the roots of the child's superego (his conscience), and strengthens his sense of right and wrong. Since, for example, the boy cannot take his father's place, he can at least become like him, eventually hoping to marry a woman similar to the one his father chose.

The child's identification is fashioned by what his parents would expect of him, rather than his personal understanding of what is right or wrong. This is in part due to the fact that much of the development of his conscience occurs automatically by identification and before his own independent judgment fully emerges. Strong identification also helps the youngster anchor his own place in the adult world. He may derive great pleasure from acting and reacting like an adult. It is an instrumental step in his becoming a civilized human being.

The child that does not identify with his parents will produce a weak superego, with weak controls over his own behavior. He may then grow up and join the other thousands of juvenile delinquents in our society.

What is worse, such people sometimes develop psychopathic personalities, in which they suffer from a total inability to separate right from wrong. They may act without conscience or superego controls. Psychopaths are often referred to as "moral imbeciles." They are quite unable to judge right from wrong.

I only mention these excesses in order to dramatize the need for us as parents to provide the kind of moral example with which our children will find it easy to identify. The Oedipal stage is as great a period of responsibility for the parent as it is for the child.

With sufficient insight, parents can respond with intelligence and understanding. Let us take the little girl who has just made an important discovery: she is different from boys by the fact of one significant omission! Not one girl, but most girls, once having discovered that boys have a genital organ which they have not, become envious and often experience uneasiness and become upset. If all this seems to some adults unnecessarily blatant and slightly perverted, let me assure them that it is nothing of the sort. On the contrary, it is experienced with the innocence and wonder of which only a child is capable.

But where do such feelings of envy and discomfort lead to? Often, the girl's anxiety may build up without the parents even being aware of it. It may never be discussed, but many parents are sufficiently sensitive to the inner turmoils of their little girls to bring this discomfort out into the open. Barring such open discussion, the typical little girl's soliloquy may go something like this: Why isn't "it" there? Will it still grow or is it gone forever? Did Mommy take it because I was bad, or because I want Daddy all to myself?

Is such self-questioning normal for a girl of Oedipal age? It is indeed. It is more typical of little girls than many of us would suppose. Some parents respond by ridiculing such thoughts and laughing them out of court. We find it much more prudent for parents to assure their little girls that "all little girls worry about these things," and that the difference now observed between herself and a little boy of her own age is quite natural and the way things were planned in the first place.

The young child's concern with sex at this age is not only a normal manifestation, but part of an important psychological process. No little girl will ever grow into a mature woman and a successful wife and mother without first having resolved her own problems of sexual identity. We only have to look about us to see women who have never resolved this very basic conflict in the very early part of life. Such women essentially reject femininity. They often pass through life in consuming resentment and jealousy of men. They often show contempt for men generally, or enter into vocational fields reserved for men. Most of them will never enter into a full and satisfying relationship with any man. If they do marry, their marriage partner is apt to be of a passive personality, with the woman remaining the dominant, aggressive partner. When such women have children, they tend as a rule to favor their sons markedly over their daughters.

Girls are not alone in this search for sexual identity. Boys show their own brand of sexual concern. Their concerns run parallel to those of girls. Girls envy what only boys can have. Boys, having it, fear to lose it. Part of this complex frequently stems from the fact that when a boy discovers that a girl does not have what he possesses, he may himself grow anxious and fearful.

Has the girl lost her penis, he may ask himself, as a result of punishment for some behavior? Was she caught masturbating? Was she angry with her parents? Such possibilities seem very real for the boy who may be really dealing with his own guilt over his hostile feelings toward his parents.

One of a parent's most common questions concerns masturbation. Rarely is the question "Should my child still be masturbating?" Most parents first want to determine whether masturbation is "normal" or "acceptable." Neither concern with the problem nor shame is called for at this stage of the child's life. Masturbation during this period, parents invariably are relieved to be told, is a perfectly normal and natural activity. Emotional problems *can* arise in this connection, but these are usually triggered by the parents' own distorted sense of guilt. Masturbation leaves absolutely no harmful effects, either physically or psychologically.

Part of this miraculous process of growing up, masturbation represents a stepping-stone to the normal sexual practices that follow. The activity itself helps develop feelings in the genital organs. If the parents now assign extreme guilt to the youngster, the child may repress the very sexual sensitivities which will later become important. In extreme cases, frigidity in the female and impotence in the male can be the result of excessive coercion and parental condemnation. In other extreme manifestations of parental interference, masturbation can become a fixed way of life, extending long into adulthood.

Even some of the best-meaning parents in the world are genuinely baffled. "Is masturbation to be overlooked entirely, or is there something we ought to say?" parents often ask. The best advice I can give is to regard masturbation during this stage on the same level as thumb-sucking in the infant, the toilet-training in the two- or three-year-old. In other words, if we can accept these habits as a temporary device for self-satisfaction, as another stepping-stone of development, proper perspective comes a bit easier.

Certainly parents should help their youngsters gain control over their impulses. When a parent can show confidence in his youngster's ability to control himself without needing to resort to parental discipline, so much the better. One invariably observes that subtle parental guidance in this respect helps to keep a youngster's masturbation at a minimum. Before too long, most youngsters learn to control their impulses, as they did their thumb-sucking and elimination.

In this as so many other human situations, coercion and ridicule by the parent will merely produce anxiety and guilt. Unhappily, the more upset and guilty a youngster may feel, the more intense and prolonged his masturbating habit may become. While there exists no single magic recipe, we usually find that youngsters with sufficient parental love and support, and an adequate number of outside interests and activities, have very little trouble in this regard.

There is a further comment to be made about the child's general interest in sex, which I think will help bring matters into focus. We are seldom worried about the child's natural interests in sex during this Oedipal period. What may worry us is the parental response to the child's interest, not the interest itself.

Now let us turn the coin: what may concern us far more is to see a child who shows *no* interest in sex at all. When we see a child who has never asked a single question about sex, we begin to wonder what is wrong. Sometimes, the answer is simple. The child's parents may have a strict policy of not having the word mentioned around the house. If that is the case, they had better change and give the child an opportunity to begin asking questions. Parents who never mention sex force the subject into the dark forbidden corners of a child's mind.

There are many opportunities in the life of a child to bring up the matter of sex in a natural way. Some mothers I know take advantage of every opportunity they can to take their youngster to see the newborn babies of family friends. Seeing a diaper changed, they find, usually provokes questions, to which answers can be readily supplied.

Children's queries about sex should always be answered. On the other hand, there is no need to go beyond the content of their questions. Answers should be supplied; no more, no less. But what sex information *is* supplied should always be factual.

Lies or fantasy never work. Even the most innocent of children finds it hard to believe that he was brought into this world on the broad wings of a stork, or that his mother found him in a cabbage patch or a flour barrel. Few parents nowadays resort to such nonsense. Yet for a child to unlearn facts about sex later in life can be a difficult and sometimes damaging process. Parents should bear this danger in mind when they make the decision on how to bring sex into some natural focus.

Fairy tales in this regard seldom pay off. To the child, simple facts of sex, and indeed, the frank description of sexual organs, are no more significant than a basketful of other assorted facts about life. The sex language of the adult is not the sex language of the very young. Ideally, the question of sex should be treated in a language of wonder, pleasure, and complete normalcy which the child can understand.

Even when parents fully recognize and agree to their roles as sex teacher and guidance counselor, they often find themselves tongue-tied in the face of the questions their children ask. "Just what should I say to Bobby about where he came from?" is a question I hear almost daily. "How did I get in your tummy, Mummy?" is another question which can drive a conscientious mother into a frenzy. These are all loaded questions. But they are loaded for the adult, not the child. No one can provide a given set of answers, because their formulation depends on the personality of both parent and child.

Whenever I am asked to help parents be specific in replying to such questions, it is rarely sufficient merely to advise directness and honesty. When we formulate an answer together, we often agree in the end that it is best to explain to the youngster that he grew in a special place inside his mother's body, and when he was big enough, he came "through an opening made especially for babies."

Most youngsters find this quite plausible and

easy to accept. But, to most children, just how they got inside their mother's body in the first place is more of a puzzle. "How did I get inside, you, Mother?" is an insistent question, usually followed by Mother suddenly developing a nervous cough.

I overheard one mother tell her six-year-old girl: "Both Mommies and Daddies have seeds inside their bodies, and when Daddy adds his seed to Mommy's when he makes love to Mommy, then a new baby may start to grow." The little girl was completely satisfied with the answer. She was grateful to her mother for sparing her all kinds of fairy tales; her mother's honesty had solved this seemingly inexplicable puzzle.

As a matter of fact, her mother's frankness was the perfect insurance against the kind of sex nonsense which her child was bound to hear from children less informed. Early enough in life, the mother establishes herself with her child as the source on sex questions. What better control and assurance could a parent possibly want?

To introduce sex to the child is to introduce life. After all else is said, it is this that the parent can impart to the child in terms which are at once basic but also touched with the divine.

Unfortunately, there remain troubled children during this period, as in all others. Difficulties which children can experience during the Oedipal period can leave their characteristic marks later on. Frequently, we find emotional disturbances in adults directly traceable to this period of life.

We all know people whose personality traits have been stamped by some earlier disturbance of their triangle of father, mother, and child. They tend to be immature, over-emotional, superficial, rarely

involving themselves deeply with anyone, demanding the impossible, and showing an excessive need
to daydream. The basic personality problem aris-
ing from the Oedipal period is in the area of sexual
identification and sexual relationships. Quite often,
a failure in the child's relationship toward his
parent-competitor as well as his parental love object can produce a general failure in his sexual
identification.

The personality of both parents as well as their
relationship with each other have a particularly
significant bearing on the child during this period.
The clues which we constantly seek in our therapy
are usually quite easy to find, whenever at least
part of the basic difficulty can be traced back to
this Oedipal phase. Is the father or mother a particularly aggressive person? Or are both parents
so passive as to cause in their child emotional
problems of an entirely different kind? All kinds
of variations in the personality patterns of the
parent are possible. We can only illustrate some
of them here.

As our first illustration, let us take Mrs. F., who
is a particularly strong and aggressive person.
These traits are just as vigorously apparent in her
role as a mother. What about her seven-year-old
boy, Kenny? What will he be like ten or twenty
years from now? We can only speculate, but unless Mrs. F. and Kenny get some help, little Kenny
may very well grow up to hate all women. We already see that Mrs. F. is imposing very rigid controls on him. What is not quite so obvious to us is
that she really doesn't want Kenny to grow up at
all. She doesn't want him to become a man. She
wants him to remain "little Kenny."

Our next case is Mr. M. In many ways, he is
like Mrs. F., hostile, aggressive, a bully in his own

home. Mr. M.'s six-year-old boy is having a tough time. He has a father who has always been hostile and domineering. Now the boy is going through all the classic symptoms of his Oedipal phase. He gives his devotion and attention to his mother. But his father-competitor was already a threatening figure long before the boy began competing for his mother's affections. What chance does he have against his father's wrath?

The boy has no inner security to fall back on. He may very well detach himself entirely from his father and regress to an overly dependent relationship with his mother. What of his later life? In adolescence as well as adult life, he will probably continue to withdraw from competition, remain fearful of all authority, and stay overly attached to his mother.

Still another reaction is possible. I have known boys who have joined forces with punitive fathers like Mr. M. and emulate their fathers' own personalities. Such boys may deny their mothers any positive feelings whatever.

What of later life? They may turn out differently, but no more successfully. They are the women haters, protecting themselves from women by their open hostility toward them.

What about passive fathers? Given a weak and ineffectual father, a boy may be frightened by the prospect of winning his Oedipal fight for his mother. Another boy may feel guilty because of what he feels is unfair competition.

I have given these examples to show to what a great extent personality abnormalities in either or both parents influence and help shape the child into an adult human being. Obviously, a successful and normal sexual identification of the youngster is best assured by having two emotionally stable parents, who accept their own sexual roles. Even stable parents do not always guarantee domestic tranquillity. Parents should accept the competitive nature of this period as a perfectly normal part of growing up. Let the child know that you love him as a little boy (or girl) and not as the grown-up man (or woman) he wants you to accept him as. These situations lend themselves to a good deal of firmness on the parent's part, which in the end will be appreciated by the child. Your firmness provides him with added security and helps control his basic instincts.

Children will chart their course with greater emotional equanimity if parents can help them verbalize their own feelings. Assure them that you experienced similar feelings of jealousy, anger, or resentment when you were young, that is, that they, too, will grow up to marry and have a wife or husband, and children of their own.

When a child loses one or both of his parents during the Oedipal phase, the effect upon his later personality development is frequently long-lasting. The Oedipal period, as we have seen, is dominated by "The Triangle." When death, war, divorce, or desertion breaks that crucial triangle, the child's emotional life can be irretrievably scarred.

What, for example, of a little girl, who has just lost her mother? The emotional cost could be high. A little girl learns many of her first feminine emotions from her mother. By observing her mother, she learns how a woman fulfills her life. Even when she plays a rivalry role vis-à-vis her mother, she learns how to handle her own feelings of competition—an important lesson in the art of adult living. The loss of a mother could provoke an unusually intense relationship with her father, which could turn into a permanent state of affairs. It may obviate her need to turn to any other man during her father's lifetime.

If the girl loses her father, the emotional cost is counted in different terms. The father's absence leaves an emotional vacuum. Deprivation of the father may turn the girl to a relationship with her mother which may have quite erotic overtones. It could be the beginnings of homosexuality; or a clinging and demanding dependency relationship. Such girls, deprived of their fathers, often turn into women incapable of forming any deep and prolonged relationships with men since they have never experienced the primary one with their fathers. Such women may go through life with revenge and anger in their hearts, with which they attempt to retaliate against what they suffered because of their fathers' withdrawal from their own lives.

This was the case of a young woman of twenty-eight whom I recently treated, cautiously—an exceptionally attractive girl. She very much wanted to marry, but her own contrary behavior patterns destroyed every such opportunity. The pattern was always the same: by her intelligence and beauty, she attracted many suitors. Invariably, she would cast them off whenever the man became serious.

When this young woman told me her own life history, the pattern became quite clear. When she was four years old her father had deserted her mother. She, too, felt deserted, and quickly absorbed her mother's sense of revenge and bitterness. Her later pattern of relating to men became in fact a means of taking out her revenge on her own father's infidelity.

In an earlier chapter, I referred to the emotional dynamics which sometimes accompany children's feelings at the time of a parent's death. Dreadful as these losses are of themselves, many a youngster's head is filled with inner guilt that the death was a direct consequence of his or her feelings of hostility toward the dead parent.

A young adolescent girl was recently referred to me, in whom these death-wish dynamics had taken on particularly compelling proportions. A whole year had gone by since Ann Marie had lost her father. Yet, she continued to be so upset, so moody and anxious, that the tragedy dominated her entire life.

Therapy with both Ann Marie and her mother soon brought out some interesting facts: Ann Marie's father, a highly successful businessman, had been well liked and respected by his business associates, but found very little use for a family life. He had in fact been a disaster as a husband and father. During her Oedipal phase, Ann Marie's disappointment in her father became a dominant strain. She grew increasingly hostile toward him. Had Ann Marie's hostility contributed to his sudden death? Ann Marie's unconscious wondered, and she never could, by herself, find a satisfactory answer. Ann Marie's mother, on the other hand, revered her husband's memory, although the marriage had in fact been highly unsatisfactory. Ann Marie could little distinguish between fact and fiction, and her emotional problems grew increasingly acute.

It will be some time before Ann Marie can resolve her deep-seated emotional conflict. Even if we consider her treatment successful, it is quite likely that some of her bitter memories will remain.

A child's deprivation of a parent need not occur by death alone. Whatever the cause, whenever the Oedipal triangle is destroyed or even disturbed, a child so affected may suffer for it long into adulthood.

I remember the case of Mr. S. who found himself in a deep depression because of his wife. For many reasons, it had been a bad marriage; in addition his wife had long been seriously ill. Mr. S. suffered from a bitter inner conflict between his desire to desert her and his guilt at the thought of forsaking her. His own mother, it seems, had literally deserted him because of her own illness. Consequently, he had been brought up in one institution after another. When it came time to marry, he picked a woman already ill with a severe heart condition. Quite possibly he chose such a woman with the unconscious desire to face his wife's pain as he had his mother's. This time, he would resolve the problem by deserting her, instead of being deserted himself.

When he faced his own hostile feelings toward his wife, he began to feel profound guilt. His guilt was the primary cause of his deep depression. Once he could see that he was unconsciously repeating his past, his own moral dilemma began to resolve itself.

I think we have seen enough youngsters and parents with emotional problems to discover one dominant strain: unless the child is able to resolve during his Oedipal period his identification toward both his parents in two distinctive ways, he may well be in for serious emotional difficulty later on. It is, I realize, often very difficult to detect such danger signs at the time they occur. Some of the people we have looked at here suffered emotionally long after they had lived through their Oedipal period. Nonetheless, the problem often began there.

There are, however, symptoms which we can

look for at the time they begin to develop. I will briefly sum them up here.

Primarily, disturbed children of the Oedipal age are sexually confused. This is to say that they are not quite sure what they want to be—boys or girls. Most boys at this age have an exaggerated fear of being physically harmed. In disturbed children, it grows into an obsession of varying intensity. In serious cases, it can become a severe handicap.

Secondly, phobias, nightmares, extreme negativism, bed-wetting are all symptoms of emotional problems of this period. At school age, learning problems are often a further indication of emotional trouble.

Many disturbed children suffer phobias generated by fears unsupported by reality. In such a child, some innocuous object in his daily environment may become the focus of his fears, which in fact represent some deeper, inner problem. Phobic-ridden children are easily given to panic and personal terror. They are difficult to treat.

Many of these emotional problems arise from some trauma in the child's background. We find that an accident, a serious illness or operation (especially one such as circumcision) can leave bad scars, particularly when they occur in the Oedipal period. Problems can often arise during one phase of life, and, failing to resolve them, the child will carry them along from one phase into the next.

Sometimes phobias stretch to proportions which I know most people would find too ridiculous to believe. Yet, anyone involved in child therapy can recite innumerable examples of children with fears which dominate their young lives to an incredible degree. Quite recently, I treated a teenage girl who suffered from fear of dogs. Just why this was she did not know. She had never been bitten or attacked by a dog, she said, and the whole thing grew into an insoluble puzzle. The very sight of a dog would send her into headlong flight.

Just like a jigsaw puzzle, however, the clues gradually took shape, and the cause of her phobia unfolded slowly in session after session. During her Oedipal phase, this girl had been intensely attracted to her father. And yet, her strong-willed and domineering mother inhibited her to the point of making her fearful of her own feelings. Then, one day, sitting in her father's favorite easy chair, she found herself fondling her father's dog. Shocked into realization that she was physically attracted to the dog, she threw it down and flew from the room. Undoubtedly, the attraction she felt during that one moment for the dog was an expression of how she really felt toward her father. Here was an example of an Oedipal problem which had remained unresolved. The girl's phobia about dogs disappeared as soon as her Oedipal conflict was recognized and solved.

Quite as common as these phobias among disturbed children in the Oedipal period are violent fits of rage. Such children are triggered into uncontrollable bursts of anger, which shock their parents by their intensity. These fits can occur at the slightest hint of frustration. The raging child can become totally uncommunicative, detach himself from the world, and turn his virulence onto himself.

If the Oedipal period proves a comparatively stormy phase for many children, it is consoling to remember that the child is also making giant strides forward in his development. The boy and girl at the end of the Oedipal period is a far cry from the baby he was at its beginning. As a matter of fact, all of this progress may leave him, as well as his parents, just a little breathless. No wonder then that during the next period of development, the latency stage, most youngsters will sit back and take a little breather. We call it a period of "consolidation."

To which many parents will gratefully say, "Thank God" and "Amen."

VI

Six Through Ten: The Widening World

AFTER REACHING the age of six, the outside world becomes the object of increasing fascination and involvement. For the normally developing child, the sixth through approximately the ninth year should pass relatively calmly. This may be news to some parents of particularly impossible eight-year-olds, but by and large we can regard this period as one of relative tranquillity.

I recall predicting such a period of relative calm and contentment to a mother of six-year-old twins. She jumped from her chair and, touched by both desperation and good humor, exclaimed: "Maybe the Good Lord planned it that way to give us poor parents a break at last!"

While she may be perfectly right, too many parents are tempted to regard this "break" as a sign to sit back and neglect some of their most important parental responsibilities. Parents face several pitfalls here. The period represents an immensely important time, for the child as well as the parent.

The years of approximately six to ten are usually referred to as they "latency period." Latency refers to something which is not visible, but which lies dormant. It is during this period that a great deal of consolidation and maturing takes place. Generally speaking, it is a period of taking stock.

The first three major periods of life, we recall

—the oral, anal, and Oedipal stages—can be quite turbulent.

Now, many of the basic conflicts lie behind your child. Most of the difficulties which are apt to crop up during the latency period represent "second rounds" of conflicts faced before.

Many parents are tempted to consider most of their rearing responsibilities now out of the way. A closer reading of this chapter, I hope, will quite readily show why parents often feel this way, and why this attitude is often regrettable. The comparative ease with which these children now take to the job of living and adjusting is not necessarily an indication of full life adjustment, but of a feeling of passivity.

For the normal child, and, let me add, for the normal parents, the latency stage opens up marvelous opportunities to come to know each other better. These opportunities never present themselves again. Adolescence arrives with puberty, and, for the child, the gates open. In a sense, the latency period is the parents' last chance to play a truly full and special role.

We have already seen how the first three stages have shaped the child. By the time the child passes into puberty, the adult is also shaped, for adult personality rarely changes radically from what we see during the latency period. The seven- or eight-year-old child, be he considerate or selfish, bullying or charming, will turn out to be virtually that kind of adult twenty years hence.

Nor is the child who has conquered the first three stages apt to encounter any serious difficulties later on—barring, of course, an unexpected trauma of unusual severity. The latency period stands in stark contrast to its predecessors: tensions now give way to calm; conflicts turn to easy adjustment; outward aggressions grow into inward introspection.

This is an excellent time for parents to take stock of their child. Is he what you hoped he would be? Is he what you might picture him to be ten or twenty years hence? If he is, much of the credit goes to you as a parent. If he is not, one still need not despair. The clay has not yet hardened. There is still time to shape it.

Let us take a further look at your child and at yourself. Has your child been able to solve all of his previous problems, his furies, and dilemmas? Do you see in him the young man or woman who has what it takes to equip him for adolescence and beyond?

One of the child's prime concerns (I might almost call it an obsession) in this period is his concern with his own adequacy or inadequacy. During the latency stage the average child will almost naturally question his own abilities. There is a wide gap between "Can I do it?" and "I *can* do it!" He is prone to be awkward, ungraceful in his walk, and perhaps sporting a pimple or two on his chin.

This is the time when the typical child will incessantly compare himself with other children of his own age. The comparisons may seem trivial, but they are nonetheless important to him. If Suzy Q. next door received a Barbie doll for Christmas, it is almost inviting a crisis if your own girl does not get the identical doll, but with more clothes, naturally! Disaster may impede unless the gap is filed at once. "Johnny's father got a color TV set. Daddy, why don't we have one?" A child's motivation rests less with the desire to acquire these things than the need to be constantly assured of his own adequacy, and, as an extension, his family's adequacy.

There is no need to cater to a child's feelings of inadequacy by loading him up with worldly goods. Quite the contrary. This is as good a time as any to provide him with the kind of emotional and spiritual balance to make him feel adequate without resort to such superficial, if understandable, comparisons. Your child's basic need in this period is to believe in himself. He should believe in his own assurance. He feels satisfied that he *can* be equal skills and his own abilities, as he can measure these by himself and in competition with others.

The child who concerns himself with a hobby— no matter how odd it may be—channels his desires to compete successfully in creative and healthful ways. If your boy has a better stamp collection than any other boy on the block, this fact alone creates a very solid basis for competitive self-assurance. He feels satisfied that he *can* be equal and superior to other boys. His own unconscious might tell him that "since I can beat anybody on the stamp collection, I *could* beat anybody on anything else, too!"

We often remind parents that we should not view these latency period activities as "foolish" or "useless." They should not be ridiculed. A five-year supply of handmade wax candles admittedly serves little worldly purpose, but to your child they may be the most beautiful and long-burning candles in the whole wide world! Many children at this age benefit immensely by getting full-hearted parental support for their projects. They may not overtly ask their parents' help for fear of divulging their own sense of inadequacy. But suggest help yourself, and see how eagerly it will usually be accepted. Who in the world but Dad, after all, knows as much about pitching softball or raising hamsters! You must help him develop enough of these skills so that he will develop the kind of self-confidence that for the boy or girl of eight or nine separates triumph from failure. A hair's breadth difference often marks one from the other.

Increasingly now, the scene of the competitive world shifts to the schoolroom. Nowhere else will the child's conviction that he "can do" have more vital and long-range implications. It is essential that he develop feelings of accomplishment in school. The entire learning process is intimately tied up with the child's having sufficient self-confidence and abilities to compete well with his classmates.

A few words about schooling in general. The whole matter of when to begin school should be looked at from the point of view of emotional readiness along with specific intellectual preparation.

Only too often we find that emotional difficulties spring from a child's experience of entering school too early, and having him unsuccessfully compete with better equipped and older children. Some children never quite get over the experience. You can help prevent such difficulties by sufficient insight into the potential pitfalls. Ask yourself whether the child is ready for school. Is he ready physically, mentally, and emotionally? What about his hearing and eyesight? Is he physically well? Does he rate satisfactorily in a reading readiness test? Does he have emotional difficulties which would interfere with his ability to concentrate? Could it impinge on his relating to the teacher or to other children?

Once in school, continued parental support is necessary. Too many parents these days abdicate all responsibilities to the school. Rarely is it possible for the teacher in the modern school setting to provide fully adequate guidance to *every* child. The teacher does what he or she can, and more often than not does it well. But the emotional aspect of the learning process is hardly all a matter of the classroom. The teacher relies on you to be a silent partner, and so does your child.

Some children have difficulties in the early grades. It is never prudent to nag the child and attempt to push him beyond his own limits of adequacy. Rather, support and encourage him, both in his schoolwork and, just as vitally, by feeding him the necessary emotional vitamins of building up his own feelings of adequacy.

I regard a basic feeling of adequacy to be as important as the very learning process itself. As adults, we are perfectly aware of the bolstering bonus of having confidence in ourselves. To be sure, we all have our ups and downs in believing in our own adequacy. But as adults, we can always reach back into our past experiences and have a fairly accurate measure of just what we are capable of doing.

Not so with the child. He has no backlog of experience to fall back on. He rarely knows just what the extent of his own adequacy may be. Nor is he going to go all out and find out unless his parents back him to the hilt and encourage him to reach out further.

Part of the child's inner conviction that "I can do" will come from the props you can prepare for him. These help to convince him that he is really as good as he secretly hopes he could be. Much of what is happening to your child during this stage develops sub-surface. You may have to dig a bit to see just what is going on. I think what you will find will be of extreme interest.

Let us take the more obvious things first. With

the end of the previous growth period the child's sexual urges usually recede. They do not disappear, but they remain repressed for the time being and kept under control. Concurrently, his ties to his parents are loosened. These ties do not necessarily weaken, but they become diffuse because of the many other strands of friendships and allegiances which the growing child now cultivates. With each new friend, his dependence on his parents becomes just a little less essential and exclusive.

In other words, all the child's drives, his relationships, as well as his tensions and conflicts, now tend to unfold outward. He looks out at the world, and the world looks at him. He needs his family's support as much as ever, but only to help him explore these wider horizons. The typical youngster of this age will thrust outward so long as he knows that he can always run home again to be reassured. Your home, in other words, gives your child that necessary base of operation from which to explore new worlds, and hopefully to conquer them. The child who feels secure with his family will far more readily try new conquests and will more readily develop a consciousness of the world around him.

Parents can best help equip their emerging child by giving him a well-developed *ego*. Not the kind that carries a chip on his shoulder, but the kind that says: "I am a growing human being of consequence." The ego is that part of ourselves of which we are always aware. It is, if you will, our concept of ourselves, of what we really are. People whom we regard as strong, stable, and capable, have strong egos; they are not egotists. Contrary to popular belief, while the child's ego begins developing at birth, it is only in this latency stage that his ego development becomes vital and acutely evident.

What exactly is involved in the development of the ego? It means that the person is beginning to control his drives and impulses. The young child with a developing ego begins to be guided by his mind, rather than by his emotions only. The Pleasure Principle, by which a child does what is most immediately pleasurable, now gives way to the Reality Principle, and his actions are more closely attuned to the realities of life.

This marks the makings of a true social being —to adjust successfully to the environment and to people around him, and to adjust to the needs of others.

The normal child is also greatly helped at this point by a rapidly developing conscience—called *superego*. The child who successfully ventured through the earlier Oedipal stage will usually have developed a well-directed conscience which will help him become a responsible human being. In short, the normal child in the latency period will have already accomplished a reasonable adjustment to life's problems, both in terms of his relation to others as well as toward his own internal emotions. This is by no means to say that these adjustments are completed. Parents who now expect their sprouting offspring to behave like adults anticipate a state of maturity which is totally unrealistic.

What of the disturbed child? While the normal child during latency develops rational behavior, the disturbed child will behave quite differently. Disturbances rise to the surface and are quite readily apparent at that age to those who are professionally trained. The troubled child usually suffers from either excessive or insufficient behavior controls. In other words, the balance wheel which controls the behavior patterns of the normally adjusted child malfunctions with varying degrees of severity.

If the disturbed child's controls are too weak, he is apt to be overwhelmed by his impulses. In other words, his emotions can run wild, and so may he. We often see children who are physically uncontrollable, who show no tolerance for even the slightest frustration, and who have a very difficult time in school and in relating to anyone around them.

We often find that such behavior disorders stem from the parents' own instability. These children are angry children. They take out their anger on their parents, at the same time fearing their parents' hostility. Their behavior creates one of those vicious circles, which even the best therapists find difficult to break. Parents of such disturbed children often generate little, if any, direction, providing no track for their children to run on. Having no controls, these children's consciences remain weak and ill-defined. Often they find it difficult to tell right from wrong. What is worse, their parents or teachers may not even point out the differences to them.

Conversely, we often run into the exact opposite in behavior patterns when the child's controls are too strong. As a result anxiety and inhibitions emerge. Such a child represses every emotion and lives constantly in fear of having his impulses run rampant and explode into the open. Such a child will probably fare better in school than his brother who suffers from too weak controls. At least, he can better manage his social relations and his schoolwork.

Both extremes, too little or too much control, are

of course highly undesirable. Only too often they leave unfortunate emotional pockmarks. Much can be done by parents themselves to prevent their occurrence. Needless to say, the earlier parents detect these emotional danger signals, the better.

Parents should make up their minds very early in the development of their children that both father and mother carry vital obligations in terms of their own involvement with their offspring. Families that work and play together, stay together. Normal children learn best by their parents' examples. Children should share their parents' enthusiasm in terms of hobbies, outside interests, and the pleasures that come from work. Both the child's growing curiosity as well as his natural aggressions are wonderfully served by projects inspired by his parents. This period is a good time to encourage Buddy to rake the leaves or have Susie help with the dishes.

Nor should material rewards always be attached. The child will soon begin to appreciate the sharing of responsibilities. Parents must also work hand-in-hand with their children to help them handle their emotions, to have them learn how to discipline their aggressions and control their tensions. This does not mean coddling them by protecting them from exposure to life's problems. On the contrary: difficulties and frustrations should be faced, but faced together. Keep in mind that children are variously equipped to handle such difficulties. If a child becomes overwhelmed by the problem, the whole point of the experience is lost. Parents, too, must steer a middle course: not too much protectiveness, not overpermissiveness, either. The child's ego must be constantly exposed and challenged. Only in this way will it develop properly.

The manner in which you handle your child during this period can be terribly important. As the parent, you must try to be reasonable and consistent in your demands, which means the setting up of certain living patterns, loose enough to allow day-to-day variations. The wise parent knows and feels instinctively his child's ego strengths as well as limitations. The parent can help the child gratify his drives by sublimating them and channeling them into useful projects. Providing a punching ball for Johnny is infinitely more satisfying than having the father become the object of Johnny's very normal physical aggressions. We usually find that these children who have had the active help and support of their parents in controlling their impulses are invariably happier children. For the six- to nine-year-old, confidence as well as a sense of freedom often result from such a cooperative effort.

The development of inner disciplines is particularly essential for success in school. Many children, while perfectly capable of doing the required schoolwork, will fall behind because they refuse to involve themselves in the learning effort. Excessive discipline usually brings a bad start to the whole educative process. Excessive freedom, on the other hand, fails to supply the child with sufficient controls.

The balance between supervision and freedom can be a sensitive one. We parents, let us be frank, like to remain the center of our child's universe— at least in the first decade or so of our child's development. But the six-year-old begins to spread his wings. He may fly out of the roost more frequently. In fact, he may visit other roosts and claim to find these more attractive than his own. As a further blow to the parents' ego, the friend's home may appear more attractive just because it is *different*. For many youngsters at this age, to be different is to be superior, since to be different is to be independent.

Independence is never total at this age. Mark Twain notwithstanding, the ten-year-old is not apt to hop the next freight West. His independence comes from having both feet firmly set on the threshold of his own home. This may seem inconsistent, but it is really not. Most children suffer from certain conflicts here—the conflict between the inner need to strike out for independence, and their still strong requirements of the continued assurance of the home.

Compromises are made, both consciously and unconsciously. He will sincerely miss his father when he is away from home, and yet literally overlook Dad's existence when he is there. He will loudly proclaim the virtues of his friend's new television set, and yet proudly invite his friends over to show off his own. He will envy his friend's repeating Colt-45, but proudly show off his own automated moon station.

Identifying with other people is not always restricted to real people. Imagination and fantasy for the six- to nine-year-old provide easy identification with characters out of books, movies, and television. This can also be a time of strong religious influences, which the child takes quite seriously. These may represent highly realistic experiences.

Identification with others also brings about immense curiosity about them. How such people live, what they talk and think about, are all objects of intense scrutiny. Curiously enough, young children at this age level tend to be extremely secretive toward their parents, while freely sharing their secrets with each other.

One reason why youngsters go to world's ends to assure that their secrets will not leak to the adult world is often their own impression that their adults have not quite "come clean" with *them* about the highly complex world they are now discovering for themselves.

What about the child's attitudes toward sex during the latency period? His interests in sex tend to shift noticeably. In the Oedipal period, sexual interest narrowed down primarily to sex differences—i.e., the little boy was different from a little girl; some dogs had "it," some had not. During the later latency stage, children are far more concerned with the basic function of sex—the ways and wherefores. For example, latency period girls become interested in pregnancy, in the reality of pregnancy and child-bearing. They play-act pregnancy by stuffing pillows under their dresses.

Except in the disturbed child, sexual fantasies will gradually diminish. Masturbation plays a less vital role. Interests in the functions of sex are normally shared with other friends of the same sex. Secrets again can be shared and held from their elders. This helps them feel more secure and more adequate. Such conduct is quite natural and should be accepted as part of the normal process of growth.

Feelings of adequacy are further assured by the different attitude they tend to show toward the opposite sex. Girls will look down their noses at boys, and boys will scoff at girls. This is the age of mutual coexistence, but also sexual segregation. While these feelings manifest themselves differently, a boy's obvious interest in girls can represent a serious devaluation of his "manliness." Girls, often still influenced by their unresolved Oedipal problems, show an "I don't care" attitude, or try to compete with boys.

In our clinical work, the particularly crucial role of the mother in respect to latency stage development is brought home to us again and again. The drive for independence may conflict with dependence on the home. Some mothers grow exceedingly anxious during this period. They become hesitant about allowing their child added freedom. Many feel them to be too young, or have insufficient trust in the judgment and maturity of the child, in the child's ability to "go it alone." Some of these fears may be entirely justified. However, the child who wants to explore the world is no longer the baby the mother thought she had. It is an end of an era, so to speak, and the start of a new one.

This path toward independence during latency is often strewn with difficulties. These ought to be easily recognized by the parents. They should not add to them. The child who experiences emotional crises at this stage may regress to an earlier dependency state. He may withdraw from social activities and cling to his mother beyond the time considered normal. Such children often develop unusually strong oral needs. Recently, for example, we saw a ten-year-old boy who exhibited an irrepressible urge to eat. The more he attempted to grow up and develop his own independent ways, the greater and more frequent became his forays to the icebox. We encouraged the mother to provide closer support, to patiently introduce him to small groups of children who would offer little competition to him. Soon he began to gain some confidence in himself, and his appetite returned to more normal proportions.

I recall another girl of nine, who suffered from

a different type of oral disturbance: This girl was sent away to boarding school, as her parents considered her overly dependent. She had clung to them like a vine, refusing to socialize with anyone on the outside. A complete separation, the parents felt, might prove the answer. But soon after entering boarding school, the child developed *anorexia nervosa*, a total inability to eat. In her own attempts to grow up and become entirely independent of her parents, she unconsciously denied her dependency by refusing any and all oral satisfactions. Such irrational reactions, I know, are hard to believe, but they happen quite often.

Overly dependent children find other means, ordinarily oral in nature, to express themselves. Some of us, I am sure, are acquainted with the child who vomits every morning shortly before leaving for school. By this simple stratagem he hopes to stay home and not be separated from his mother.

School phobias can develop to such extremes that vomiting becomes but one of the symptoms. Anxiety-ridden youngsters can be driven by many demons: Fear of the teacher, of school in general, or of hostile classmates. I recall eight-year-old Billy, who came to our clinic for treatment of a serious school phobia. Just before schooltime each morning, Billy would vomit violently and break into uncontrollable hysteria. The underlying cause turned out to be a fairly common one. Only recently, Billy's mother had had a second baby. Billy reacted to the new baby with intense rivalry. The prospect of giving up his mother for a new baby brother after eight years of possessing her entirely became too much to accept. It created more anxiety than he was able to bear. Our therapy focused on Billy, and it soon became clear to him that the arrival of a newborn brother did not exclude him from his own full share of love and attention.

Such phobias can also be aggravated by the parents. I recently treated Teddy, a boy of six. His problems began soon after entering first grade. But the problem turned out to be more his mother's than Teddy's: Because of her own difficult childhood as well as unhappy marriage, she became so dependent on Teddy for satisfying her emotional needs that she found it almost impossible to give him up. The daily separations upset her. She also feared Teddy's possible transfer of loyalty to his new teacher. It was not long before he began to absorb his mother's anxiety, and vomiting and emotional outbursts followed. In time, therapy with Teddy's mother helped clear up her anxieties.

Seen in terms of the shaping of the final personality structure of your child, you will find yourself more or less in the last stretch during the latency period. There are two very excellent reasons why you as the parent should involve yourself a great deal in your child's life during this formative period. First of all, it represents your last great chance to help shape his emotional structure in an appreciable way. With adolescence comes a cutting loose of the hitherto close ties between yourself and your child. Secondly, the child's curiosity and intellectual capacities normally develop to a higher degree during latency than during his earlier years. He is highly receptive to new ideas and patterns of life.

Long after the latency period is passed, the kind of emotional building blocks laid during this period will largely determine the human qualities of this new generation.

VII

The Early Teen-ager

ADOLESCENCE, as one childhood authority so aptly puts it, begins "when the nicest children begin to behave in a most awful way."[1]

I like this approach because it contains both a sense of reality as well as humor—two vital ingredients for a sane approach on the part of parents to their teen-age offspring and the entire span of adolescence.

In dealing with adolescents' problems, I have often observed that some parents act as though adolescence were happening to them, and not to their sons and daughters. Enough nonsense has been written about adolescence to strike cold terror into the hearts of all too many parents. Other parents tend to slide slowly into some sort of merciful comatose state, from which they do not reemerge until this fearsome period lies safely behind.

I happen to believe that adolescence doesn't lend itself to suffering alone, but to a good deal of enjoyment for both generations involved. From all evidence at hand, the vast majority of parents come through the ordeal surprisingly unscathed. Their laughter may take on a slightly hysterical edge, but it is nevertheless laughter.

Adolescence lasts for about eight to ten years. While we can generalize on some matters about the whole range of adolescence, there obviously also exist many distinguishing characteristics from one child to the next, and also within every child from his early to late adolescence.

If we begin to approach the adolescent period with some roadmap in hand, the various phases of teen-age behavior and emotionality may fall more easily into place. The first period is usually referred to as *preadolescence* or *puberty,* and usually occurs between the ages of eleven and thirteen in girls and thirteen to fifteen in boys. For both, *early adolescence* takes over for the next two years. In the next chapter, we will pay particular attention to *middle adolescence,* which covers the ages of fifteen to eighteen in girls and seventeen to nineteen in boys. A girl's *late adolescence* ranges from eighteen to twenty-one years of age, and in boys from nineteen to twenty-one.

Adolescence represents the sometimes rocky roadway from childhood to adulthood. There is no other way to get there. Taken point to point, from the eleven-year-old child to the college-age young adult, a whole world of change helps shape and etch the permanent personality features of the young person.

Most of these changes, ranging over a period of eight to ten years, occur relatively calmly and are marked by only mild and temporary disturbances. Adolescents with more severe conflicts who pass through these years of change with violence and extreme behavior vacillations are neither normal nor typical.

Yet the impression persists that adolescence must inevitably be marked by long years of discontent, fraught only too often with drama, fireworks, and perhaps unspeakable crises. Today's teen-ager and the wide variety of conflicts which seem to affect him have become the focus of almost continuous national debate. This period of life produces the highest incidence of juvenile delinquency, and there are many well-meaning people who use the words "adolescence" and "juvenile delinquency" almost interchangeably. Terror strikes their hearts when confronted by either term.

Not long ago a very worried mother came to see me, to talk about her eleven-year-old son. It seems that he had all of a sudden become very difficult. When I tried to reassure her and suggested the possibility of oncoming adolescence, she reacted as if struck by a bolt of lightning.

That mother's reaction to adolescence is not at all uncommon. Adolescence, that half-adult, half-child period, is a serious matter both for the adolescent as well as his parents and society. We can hardly look adolescence straight in the eye without becoming emotional about it.

Perhaps, today, the distance from childhood to adulthood which adolescents must travel is longer than it has ever been before. Increasingly, our adult world turns out to be less and less that of our childhood and the childhood of our children. The adjustment comes slowly and often with some difficulty. Where adjustment is not made successfully, where some part of the child's adapting mechanism goes out of order, abnormal behavior and juvenile delinquency often result. But we should be careful not to confuse the two. Some parents find it difficult to understand that while juvenile delinquency is a frequent abnormal behavior disorder of adolescents, it is *not* a natural consequence of the child's being an adolescent. This distinction is important.

I would not want to understate the serious extent of juvenile delinquency. Some seven hundred thousand children annually are now taken into our courts, and delinquency has grown into a national cancer that gnaws at the very fiber of our society. While the number of juvenile delinquents is appalling, let us also remember that there are over twenty million adolescents in this country, the vast majority of whom pass through these years without overt anti-social behavior. It is true that they may very well subscribe to an American sub-culture, but their allegiance to it rarely lasts beyond their teen-age years.

The very size and national spread of delinquency make many parents abdicate their most important responsibilities toward helping guide their teenager through this choppy sea. There are a number of reasons for parents' failure to take a strong and guiding hand in the destiny of their youngsters.

The frequent discussions I have with parents convince me that many of them fear the prospect of being called a "square" by their adolescent youngsters. This prevents them from taking the kind of active and decisive role which could prevent much of the current chaos in our suburbs, on our highways, and at our neighborhood street corners. Many parents seem to have no idea how to handle their adolescents. They are not at all sure what may be considered normal rambunctious adolescent behavior, and at what point it spills over into deviate behavior.

Unfortunately, for all our national concern about delinquency, we know far more about its unhappy manifestations than we do about its precise cause. Despite some important and weighty pioneering studies in the field, we are only beginning to predict delinquency with any degree of certainty. It remains a social cancer, and like cancer, its causes are still little understood. Its cure comes frequently too late and sometimes demands desperate measures.

Many parents prepare for the adolescence of their children long before their offspring are scheduled to reach this fearsome age. By the time of their own Waterloo the anticipated molehill has grown into a forbidding Mount Everest. By this time also, some parents have sunk to such a dismal state of anticipation, that frequently they and not their children require our help. Why do youngsters behave so badly, parents often ask?

Their behavior, as we might suspect, is the result of a complex series of changes and adjustments which strike at the very essence of their young lives. Such changes occur during a period of genuine emotional upheaval. Intense emotionality and depth of feeling emerge to a larger degree during adolescence than at any other point in a lifetime.

Adolescence is not a new phenomenon. Huckleberry Finn, we will recall, was not exactly a timid, domesticated Lord Fauntleroy. Adolescents of yesteryear ran away from home, stowed away on a boat to America, or hit the trail to the Wild West. Adventure beckoned everywhere. Today's frontiers have changed, but the drives and turmoil of adolescents remain.

The end of World War II saw a rise in juvenile delinquency all over the world. Born of poverty and broken homes throughout much of the civilized world, delinquency has also ironically multiplied because of the opposite manifestations of affluence, leisure time, and overabundance. The war-torn orphans of yesterday have often become the spoiled adolescents of today. If we have a higher incidence of delinquency in this country, it is due in part to the fact that we have affluence and overabundance in greater measure than anywhere else.

This, of course, is not the whole picture. Large

numbers of teen-agers have declared "war on society," as a national magazine put it recently. But the war on society remains basically part of the innumerable skirmishes which youngsters exercise individually within themselves. The teen-ager in turmoil will declare war upon himself as well as on the world.

When the child crosses into the land of the teen-ager, both his internal world as well as the world about him change rapidly. Some can cope with such rapidity; others cannot. Those teen-agers who cannot adjust to the new rules of the game try to make their own rules as they go along. This is how the teen-age cult is born, and why it flourishes in its very isolation.

To many parents, the world of the adolescent looks unreal and quite unfathomable. Many of us look upon our youngsters' behavior with some bemusement, and perhaps with just a little incomprehension. Still too few parents make any attempt whatever to take the time and imagination necessary to put themselves into the world of their adolescent sons and daughters. For most of us, our own adolescence has receded too far into the past to recall the way things appeared to us then. Adolescence tends to take on an unreal and alien quality quite soon after the teen-ager passes on into his twenties. The universe of the adolescent and the universe of the responsible young adult are different constellations, even though separated by a very few years.

What we must remember is that all the years of adolescence are marked by a long series of uncertainties. When the uncertainties of growing up are further compounded by the contemporary uncertainties of our present fragile or fractured world, traditional and established patterns can become easily clouded and quite beyond the reach of the teen-ager. The youngster who under the best of life's circumstances is worried about his manhood, his complexion, his ability to compete in school and college is in double jeopardy when his gnawing concerns extend to the possibility of being drafted and serving abroad.

Thus, uncertainty of a multiple nature characterizes much of adolescent life today. A long list would be necessary were we to name all of the uncertainties which beset young people. They are mostly bound up in uncertainties of a changing relationship with ourselves as parents. For the first time in his young life, you should remember, your child must by himself find the answer to many of these crucial questions. You are no longer the crutch upon which he has up to now leaned every step of his way. The crutch is discarded. He stands on his own. He may still stagger a little. You may hold ready a cushion, which will come in handy if he does fall. But a cushion is never a crutch.

It is here, in the process of the teen-ager's need to discard the parental crutch, that much of the trouble begins. It can prove highly frustrating to both youngster and parent. And yet, the normally developing youngster must now begin to declare his independence. The onset of adolescence also becomes the point of no return. It is here that the life paths of parent and child begin to branch apart. It is at this time that parental inability to cope with and control a youngster becomes a point of frequent concern.

It seems a common failing of parents that they concentrate too much on the gaps between themselves and their adolescent children rather than focus on the children themselves. The gap is far less important than the direction and nature of the adolescent's own development. Here again, I find that many parents tend to confuse cause and effect. The separation between mother and father and child is not the nub of the problem. It is rather the inability of one or both parties to recognize the existence of two paths, two worlds, two sets of interests, and so concentrate instead on the strong common bonds of family, tradition, and love that bind them together.

Many parents, of course, recognize these two spheres of the adolescent and the "normal" world, but they are unable to bridge the two either by act or by word. "I just can't reach my boy anymore" is a so often repeated expression of frustration that one can almost predict the tale of failure before the parents open their mouths.

Frequently, parents pin the whole blame of their failure to "break through" to their youngsters on themselves. If this is your feeling, it would be well to point out that many teen-agers are so totally encased in their own armor of adolescence that they can neither be talked *to,* talked *at,* or talked *with.* The teen-ager (being a "good" child) may be physically there to listen, but precious little will filter through. In a recent survey of over 5,500 high school seniors, only one in ten boys and one in five girls always talked over his personal problems with a parent. About half of these 5,500 youngsters occasionally shared their problems with their parents, while one in every four pointedly stated that they seldom, if ever, took their problems to their elders.

Parents who complain to us that their adolescent youngster *seems* like a different person are really not far from wrong. In very significant ways, he *is* different. The second decade of life is filled with so many basic new developments that life indeed changes, both physically and emotionally. At no other comparable period do physical changes come so rapidly as during adolescence.

I believe that still too few parents appreciate the profound changes taking place in those few years. We have all known boys who have shot up half a foot in a year. To feed the new "giant" takes an appetite and a quantity of food with which his body often cannot cope. His skin breaks out in blemishes; and other symptoms of poor nutrition or inadequate digestion are also common occurrences. Sexual organs develop more rapidly and body hair begins to grow. Girls develop breasts, and boys' voices become men's. The physical changes come fast and often furiously. Only rarely are they matched by comparable emotional maturity. Adolescent boys are full-grown men with children's emotions; girls, turned into women, are still ill equipped emotionally to cope with womanhood.

Internal physiological changes in the adolescent are just as vital as the external changes. But being internal, they can be easily overlooked and thus little appreciated by parents for the important part they play in their effect on teen-age behavior.

The new and more active functioning of the endocrine glands in the puberty child creates vital body changes of high significance. Hormones, which these endocrine glands secrete, enter the bloodstream and in turn activate all the other glands. Hormonal balance may not be achieved for some time. In the interim the imbalance may cause in the teen-ager abrupt changes in his physical and emotional state. These result in feelings of well-being alternating with depression and anxiety.

Such wide swings from euphoria to depression are particularly acute in the girl. With the beginning of ovulation, the girl's body functions produce particularly strong strains and stresses, which each girl must work out in her own way. The boy, on whom puberty falls with somewhat less weight, becomes nonetheless acutely aware of his own sexuality, and he grows increasingly sensitive to sexual stimuli.

Boys' tensions normally are relieved by nocturnal emissions. Release of tension by masturbation is common among adolescents and is a habit almost universally practiced. In Chapter V we discussed the way parents should handle this situation. In adolescence particularly, great care should be exercised not to produce additional guilt in the youngster. A relaxed talk by an understanding father will usually do more to reassure some of the adolescent's basic uncertainties and insecurities than the more thoughtless course of some parents who warn their children of the dire consequences of masturbation—all of which are totally untrue.

These important endocrine changes leave their mark on the youngster in a great variety of ways. A teen-ager will often show such excessive fatigue as to be almost abnormal. He often exhibits an inordinate hunger, which seems never to be satisfied. These hormonal imbalances may have an emotional impact: adolescent behavior is marked by irritability, sudden anger, often by extreme restlessness. Some adolescents are caught in perpetual motion. The only way to keep these youngsters in a chair for more than a minute at a time would be to put a harness on them.

The physical awkwardness of the early adolescent, whose legs may be growing at a different rate than his chest, also contributes to general emotional instability. From the emotional standpoint, these differences come unhappily just at the wrong time. It is precisely during adolescence that he most fears to be different. Because he finds himself shooting up like a beanpole, the teen-ager is often apt to lose much of his sense of belonging, and he tries to rid himself of this in the anonymity of a group. He does not want to be an individual. He has intense cravings to be like everyone else. Joining a group provides the necessary escape from himself which only the group can provide. Most adolescents gather reassurance by replacing their weak individual identity by strong group identity.

But even within the safety of his group, the typical adolescent—frightened, perplexed, and uncertain of what the future may bring—cannot escape the thought that for him life may have come apart at the seams. Nonetheless, this period of chaos and disorganization is necessary in the final shaping of the adult personality. Childhood patterns must inevitably be dropped or destroyed before full adult maturity can be attained.

When I look back at all of the adolescents with whom I have worked, I often wonder if there is not some little sign that flashes in the back of their minds, warning "Last chance before maturity." I suspect that they are desperately afraid that their lives and personalities will inexorably harden into concrete once adolescence has passed.

This "last chance," of course, is often played out over a prolonged period of years. From the parents' point of view, perhaps the most appalling thing about adolescence is that it lasts so long. "It's a long haul," one father said to me not so long ago. He was not at all sure that he was going to make it. The most reassuring thing I could tell him was that his child was going to make it even if he was not.

From the parents' point of view, early adolescence may produce seemingly more puzzling phenomena than the older, full-fledged adolescent. The reasons for this are many, and they could easily traumatize the unknowing parent. A very obvious one, of course, is that the early adolescent may still appear to be a child in almost every physical sense. Seeing little visible change, parents naturally assume that nothing has really changed. A parallel assumption is then almost automatically made that any emotional changes could therefore be little more meaningful. Their assumptions can be wrong on both counts.

We witness another interesting phenomenon in the early adolescent: In many young teen-agers, we once again see some of the more classic childhood habits, which we expected to have been given up permanently some years before. Now they may crop up again, for the last time. Once again, we may come across irregular eating habits, silly antics, nightmares, and outbursts of fearful imaginations. In most cases, these behavior patterns are purely transient, to be discarded forever. Parents need not worry that somehow the clock mechanism has reversed itself.

What can be said about typical behavior of the early adolescent? There is first of all no doubt that this period marks the beginning of the child's "casting off." He will be less and less around the house from now on. He is also apt to communicate less and less. His increasingly longer absences from home will be spent in the company of other young people, whom he or she will openly, and sometimes rather cruelly, prefer to your own company. Many parents seem to feel that this drawing away means that their youngsters' love and affection for them must also be on the wane. In most cases this is simply not true. The nature and character of the relationship may change, but it is not in any sense about to come to an end.

There are more influences at work here than just that of the youngster and the parent. The casting-off process is not entirely voluntary on the youngster's part. Although it is true that some parents' unbending attitudes drive their youngster further away, most early adolescents are driven to broader horizons by their increasing need for self-identification and the multiple appeals and attractions of the outside teen-age world. The casting-off usually entails considerable emotional turmoil, which the parent is only rarely aware of. The preadolescent's need to pull away from his parents is often accompanied by considerable pain and guilt of his own. Yet, he must inevitably face the shift. He will often willfully hide his lifelong affection and cover his emotions by a conscious, studied, and total indifference.

Parents, in fact, must have a pretty strong ego of their own to come through this period emotionally unscathed. The person who has always harbored some doubts about his or her ability as a parent may very well be totally crushed by the abrupt turning away of his adolescent children. This may hold true especially for the parent and the adolescent of opposite sex. Adolescents must make major adjustments in their sexual drives, and their relationship to their parents can be vitally affected.

To illustrate, a typical adolescent boy may well become wary or fearful of his feelings toward his mother. Conversely a girl will become cautious in her showing of affection for her father. The reasons are easily understood. Sexual drives and desires are gradually being developed, but their effective control is still uncertain. The adolescent has sexual urges which he must not permit himself to have toward his parent. His defense is one of feigned indifference, sometimes brutally expressed. It is important for the parent to realize that such indifference is often designed to cover up the closest and most basic affection for the parent.

We sometimes see these inner drives and fears expressed in interesting clinical manifestations. Recently, a mother brought in her fifteen-year-old daughter, who unaccountably took to vomiting without any apparent physical cause. Ursula appeared to be healthy and, on the surface at least, a well-adjusted teen-ager. Her inexplicable vomiting related to her feelings toward her father, who showed her great affection and attention. These feelings proved to be the cause of the vomiting. The well-meaning father had continued to have the kind of close physical contact which might be regarded as perfectly normal when his daughter was eight or ten. But at the age of fifteen, this contact could trigger sexual desires, which she knew she must avoid at all cost. Thus each time Ursula's father showed physical affection for his daughter nausea and the threat of vomiting would make the girl dash out of the room, leaving behind a puzzled and irritated father. Once I had explained to him the dynamics of the situation, he became much more reserved in the ways he expressed his love. Soon the vomiting stopped.

There can be many variations on this theme. I have known many fathers who quite innocently walk into a hornet's nest of emotions. I recall fifteen-year-old Susie, who had throughout her

early life enjoyed a close relationship with her father. Susie's mother was a frigid woman, and the
father was both emotionally and sexually starved.
It was therefore quite natural for Susie's father to
find at least some emotional balance by maintaining a closeness of feeling which Susie (after puberty) found increasingly disturbing. Her solution lay in totally denying her heterosexual role.
She retreated into a harmless pseudohomosexual
relationship with a girl friend. Once we had helped
the father understand the dangers of excessive
physical contact with his daughter during her maturing years, the problem almost solved itself.
Susie's relationship to her father continued to be
warm and affectionate, but on a less physical basis,
while her own interest in her girl friend gradually
waned into obscurity.

The adolescent's concern with his sexuality is
one of the cornerstones of teen-age behavior. It
takes many forms. Much of it is done with great
hesitation, an almost total lack of self-assurance,
and frequently forebodings, which the adolescent
takes great pains to hide. It is in preadolescence
that young people first become fully aware of their
masculinity and femininity. During these years the
teen-ager's sexual interest remains mostly confined
to his own sex. This is why young girls will be
attracted to groups of other girls, while boys will
pretty much stick to boys. Any mingling with the
other sex is more easily and safely conducted in
large groups instead of individually.

Most parents are grateful for small favors.
However, I know of some who are frightened by
this pseudohomosexuality. Some disturbed fathers have told me of their shock at seeing their
daughters go off arm in arm with their girl
friends. They could already foresee ruined lives

before the girls had finished high school.

Girls, particularly at this age, will invent an astonishing number of reasons to get together with other girls. Parents often ask me whether they ought to let their daughters join a slumber or pajama party. I remember one father particularly muttering "God knows *what* goes on at those slumber parties!" The way he said it suggested at the very minimum the smoking of marijuana and an orgy of unspeakable depravity.

The fact is that the majority of early adolescents could not be less interested in such goings-on. The thrills come rather from a tussle or two on the floor and the accurate aim of a pillow in a girl friend's face. A slumber party, in other words, is a harmless way in which teen-age girls spend time together and have fun. Where some parents fall down is in not being more careful of the kind of children their youngsters go around with, and the kind of homes in which these get-togethers take place.

Remember also that, for the moment, we talk of the girl who is eleven or thirteen, and the boy of thirteen to fifteen. Their relationships among their own sex are totally harmless and normal at this age. It is only in the later stages of adolescence that the opposite sex begins to hold for most of them even the slightest genuine attraction. Even then, such sexual interest as there is will often be expressed in a very superficial fashion. The kind of relationship that can cause problems is the one which takes place in secret and far away from the eyes of observing adults. But this is rarely a worry in the case of the early adolescent.

The very children who in their childish innocence flirt around the borderline of sex are also the ones in whom feelings of guilt imposed by stern parents can change their entire outlook on sexuality. Parental prohibition may arouse a kind of unhealthy curiosity about sex, quite absent heretofore.

Parents and society, of course, may contribute to precocious sexuality. Dating of nine- or ten-year-olds nowadays seems to be considered all right by some parents. The ten-year-old girl who is squired around by a twelve-year-old boy-wonder is often provoked into a sexual identification which is far too premature and was probably not of the youngster's design in the first place. The premature use of lipstick, nail polish, teased hair, and high heels is psychologically unsound and denies the child the all-too-brief innocence of childhood.

The temptation of some parents literally to catapult their teen-agers into adulthood is better understood if we have a closer look at what is going on in the minds of the parents. By the time children become teen-agers, parents, and especially mothers, may detect in their growing youngsters their own aging. During these teen-age years many mothers will unconsciously attempt to close the age gap between themselves and their daughters by making themselves feel, look, and act as youthful as possible, while making their daughters appear and act older.

The mother-daughter relationship may thus evolve into a twin-sister relationship. This relationship may temporarily prove reassuring to the mother, but it can never serve any sound purpose from the point of view of the daughter. Fathers, too, are sometimes tempted to read more maturity into their teen-age sons than is merited. A father will often try to recapture his lost youth by playing left field on his son's baseball team. This does no harm, so long as the father remains a father and does not confuse his own identity with his son's.

In actuality, all of these mother-daughter and father-son partnerships have a rather hollow ring, because rivalry at this age is far more characteristic than a twin-sister relationship. By the time the child reaches early adolescence, he is prone to become jealous, competitive, and occasionally resentful of his parents. Mothers particularly often have a difficult time with their early teen-age daughters. The going can get to be quite turbulent for both of them.

Even though this usually plays itself out at the unconscious level, the teen-age girl can be forced into almost constant conflict. She will desire her mother's protection at the same time that she attempts to create her own individuality by being critical of her. Such ambivalence obviously leads to conflict.

The mother often gets the worst of the bargain, since these tensions and frequent upsets exist at a more conscious level in the adult than in the teenager. Many a mother tends to compound the problem by trying to clamp down her feelings of frustration and the occasional fits of anger that are bound to crop up. It is far more advisable for her under such circumstances to release her anger. If she finds herself under such pressures she should express them openly. Her daughter will find her a more real person. Both parent and child should accept such occasional explosions. Acceptance of them makes for a happier coexistence. Facing up to frustrations is always healthier than total repression.

Boys, as well as girls, undergo their own crises of adolescence. From a very early age, most boys are taught how to assert themselves and protect themselves against the aggression of others. By the time they reach their teens, boys are normally highly conscious of the possible hostilities about them. They are apt to be more fearful of such threats, as well as of the possibility that their fears may be discovered by others. Many boys, in order to maintain status among their own age groups, successfully manage to suppress such fears among other boys, but readily admit to them in the privacy of their own homes.

Normally, a mother's response to such fears differs from the father's: Mothers tend to become overprotective and concerned. They may encourage some additional dependence on the part of their children during this period. Fathers, on the other hand, often become irritated and annoyed. They tend to push their boys into masculine independence, for which the youngsters are not yet prepared. Both the mother's overprotectiveness and the father's rejection are of course extreme reactions. They can only hamper the emotional growth of a child who is floundering about in search of himself.

Adolescence is not a period of all white and all black, but varying shades of gray. Parents should be grateful that this is so. If the adolescent were to solve his various conflicts totally by one extreme or the other, the awkwardness of the adolescent could well become the awkwardness of the adult as well. In reality, the entrance into adulthood is the result of innumerable compromises along the way. One of the key conflicts, certainly, is that of the adolescent's family versus his group, or gang. The overly protective mother may keep the boy from joining the group and assure his spending all of his free time by her side, while the forceful ejection by the father may indeed throw the youngster into the center of group activity, but accompanied by the total rejection of his home. Parents who are aware of just how these teen-age conflicts operate will therefore wisely work toward some middle position.

I know that many parents divide the world of their adolescent into the world of the family and the world of their friends. While these at first may seem antipodal, both are essential elements in adolescent development. The normal adolescent will rarely choose one exclusively over the other, unless he is forced into it. The group to which he belongs, while often creating real headaches for the parent, represents to him a vital necessity. He may opt for his group, even if this means going against his parents. The more parents reject the group and criticize the youngster's friends, the more they thrust their youngsters totally into the lap of their group.

But the normal adolescent needs both the warmth and security of his own home as well as the homogeneity of his group. Many parents make the mistake of forcing a choice. If they do they will place their children in terrible dilemmas and create additional emotional hazards.

To recognize that adolescent life requires these dual loyalties is the first step. The second step requires parents to treat their teen-agers with the respect and sensitivity which is due any person who in six to eight years will be fully adult. Punishment of the teen-ager is just as necessary as punishment for the smaller child. But the manner in which it is carried out is of vital importance to the adolescent. So long as the relationship continues to run on a solid track of respect and mutual trust, the occasional breakdowns that require discipline will not hurt. The worst accusation a teen-ager can hurl at his parents is that they are treating him like a child. The normal adolescent will not resent discipline, only the manner in which it is meted out.

Also at stake here is an increasing sharing of decision-making and responsibilities. Obviously, the sixteen-year-old boy is entitled to have a greater share of determining the daily issues of life than the twelve-year-old. As we shall see in the following chapter, the older adolescent is apt to take a different view of his home relationships, as he increasingly moves away from the family constellation.

1 Dr. Fritz Redl: *Pre-adolescents*, Child Study Association of America, 1943.

VIII

The Maturing Adolescent

Adolescents, though kicking and screaming,
    And often with ghastly results,
In time lose the battle, becoming
    The thing they've most hated: adults.

                RICHARD ARMOUR

PARENTS, who have put into the bank years of love, attention, and respect for their child, can count on keeping reasonable control in advanced adolescence, just as in early adolescence.

I can cite a vast number of youngsters of such inner resources that one would never need to fear either for them or the friends they select for themselves. Many of the most outstanding teenagers I know come from homes whose parents have for years provided them the utmost leeway and flexibility of action, and also love, respect, and confidence. No matter what shape the world may be in, it is on these cornerstones that successful human beings continue to be built.

As the adolescent grows older, the pattern and style of parental treatment become even more important. Adolescent may alternate from the gang or group to their own family hearth, but nothing can be as important to them as the secure knowledge that, at home, they amount to something, and that the family regards them at an almost adult level. Although most youngsters may never admit it, being taken in on family confidences, being asked advice, sharing in both the material and emotional life of their parents means something precious and vital.

Just how a youngster handles himself through the difficult adolescent period is really centrally related to the nature of his relationship to his parents.

Let me illustrate: Recently, I had occasion to observe a group of fifteen- and sixteen-year-old girls engaged in a discussion on parents. What they said about them as well as about themselves says a good deal about their adolescent behavior patterns as well. Some of them, who considered themselves "swingers," denied categorically that their parents meant anything to them. "Aren't *all* mothers always crabbing and whining and yelling," said one, "and aren't all fathers old fuddy-duddies?" Some nodded with approval. But one blurted out, "It doesn't *have* to be that way!"

The latter, I think, spoke for a larger number of adolescents than some of us realize. This particular girl regarded her mother as her best friend. The cardigan she was wearing, she said, was her mothers', and all her friends had been envious of the way she looked. That girl's mother, of course, was a wise parent in helping her daughter feel secure about herself.

There are many such parents, and they help their adolescent offspring in myriad ways. Never do they do it condescendingly, but always as one equal to another. In fact, it is sufficient for most youngsters to know that such support and advice is forthcoming, if asked for. Parents who have built up a good inventory of companionship and support through their children's earlier years rarely have difficulty in impressing on them in later years that this support and understanding continues to be there for the asking.

Parental support in adolescence shows itself in many ways. Parents ought to be sensitive to what should not be said and done, as well as what should be readily expressed. Interference should be held to a minimum. Parents must be able to make allowances for adolescent behavior. Issues which at other times would be regarded a small matter loom to seemingly immense importance.

Tom R. was referred to me because his parents had fallen into the common trap of belittling an issue which to Tom, a sixteen-year-old, seemed terribly important. For some time Tom had with great vehemence insisted on having his own room, into which he was prone to disappear for long periods. Tom's house happened to be a large one. There was no trouble about finding a room for him. Tom's parents acceded, but insisted that no boy of his age had a right to lock himself up behind closed doors. They demanded that the door of his room be kept open. When the boy continued to close his door contrary to their wishes, the father moved all of Tom's belongings to his brother's room during one of his weekend absences, which settled the matter for the father. But not for Tom.

A week later Tom ran away from home and in time turned up with an uncle four hundred miles away. It was difficult for Tom's parents to understand that an adolescent's need for privacy can amount to a passion. Most teen-agers feel a growing need for privacy. Parents should provide such facilities, whenever feasible. To the teenager, to have a room all to himself, which can be barred to the "outside" world, provides a special meaning, and is central to the search for his own identity.

The question of privacy, of course, goes beyond the confines of a boy's room. Parental questions, posed as a point of natural family interest, frequently are regarded as prying by the typical adolescent. It is almost as though he wishes hermetically to seal off his own manner of life. It is best under most circumstances to leave well enough alone. Questions will only get answers when the adolescent is in the mood to answer. It will do no good to press if any reasonable answer is to be expected. These are delicate human equations, and wise parents will play the game as they go along. They should certainly exert control whenever this becomes necessary and whenever it is possible. However, it ought not to be attempted unnecessarily.

If this sounds contradictory, it is perhaps no more so than the adolescent mood itself. Most normal youngsters will unconsciously welcome the presence of parental control. It makes them feel safer and more secure in handling their own uncertain impulses. On the other hand, there remains much surface resentment of overt parental assertion. During the child's adolescent period there should be an awareness of parental power, rather than its overt expression.

Parents often forget that as the adolescent years go by, their control and influence take on different shapes and forms, still potent, but changed. Characteristic of the age, I suppose, is the fact that a good majority of parents who come to us with problem adolescents tell us that the use of the family car was the first bone of contention. A car has a special meaning for todays' teen-ager.

"It is almost impossible to overestimate the symbolic value of the automobile to the adolescent male," writes Dr. Henry D. McCay, of the Institute for Juvenile Research. "Its possession and use is a symbol of adulthood. It is a mechanical device in an era which stresses mechanics. In use it represents power, speed, excitement, freedom from restraints, and a distinct mode of self-expression. And an automobile is almost an absolute necessity for dating."[1]

Coupled with the question of the use of the family car is the adolescent's next logical request, which is to have a car of his own. Bowing to the almost inevitable, many parents who are financially able to do so succumb. This solution does avoid a good deal of family squabbling, and the family car remains under full family control, and more likely in one piece. Many parents find it hard to adjust to this idea. Why does their youngster appear in such a desperate need of an automobile when they themselves felt no such need during their own childhood? Without lapsing into value judgments, suffice it to say that times have changed. The automobile has just about taken over adolescence, if adolescence has not already taken over the automobile.[2]

My own feelings are sharply at odds with what now seems generally accepted as broad national custom. No youngster, in my opinion, should own and operate his own car, unless it is wholly paid for and maintained out of his or her own earnings. All too many parents are nowadays caught in the web of providing cars for their youngsters because their next-door neighbor gave one to *his* son last Christmas. This kind of gift creates easy virtues and false value judgments, which subsequently become difficult to erase. Both privileges and property must be earned and worked for. Too many parents give in to their teen-age youngsters with consequences which rarely work out well for the parents or the youngsters themselves.

Parents should be adamant in their insistence that the laws be respected and, should the boy or girl get into trouble, parents should make no effort to bail the culprit out. The teen-ager has legal responsibilities and under no circumstances should he be allowed to rely on a good-hearted parent to get him out of trouble.

One of my patients, a seventeen-year-old boy, had been heavily fined three times within a six-month period for reckless driving. His license was about to be taken away. His parents asked me to write a compassionate letter to the courts, stating that the young man had been under "emotional stress" while committing these misdemeanors. I refused. The boy's dilemma was essentially his parents' fault. Had they earlier taught him strict obedience to the law and impressed upon him the meaning of responsibility, the boy would undoubtedly have behaved quite differently.

As the youngster's spheres of activity widen, so does the nature of parental control. Besides the use of a car, parents begin to face a host of other decisions: They must for instance decide how long a time—a night, a long weekend—their teen-agers should be allowed to stay away from home. Whether or not they feel free to permit long absences will depend upon the youngster's basic sense of responsibility and the quality and habits of his group.

What about drinking and smoking, many parents ask? It would be easy to say that it is best not to. However, teen-age smoking is now highly prevalent, and seems here to stay. Many adolescents smoke, either openly or in secret. My own opinion is that it should happen in full view. Then, at least, if such smoking is excessive, parents can try to do something about it. Excessive smoking in an adolescent may be a sign of tension and stress with which the teen-ager cannot deal alone. He may need to have the help of his parents or the help of a professional person. In my own view, youngsters should be strongly urged by their parents not to begin smoking at all.

Alcohol rarely poses a hazard for a child in a family where drinking is not a problem. A family of non-drinkers or mild social drinkers is not apt to produce a juvenile alcoholic. It is also better for the youngster to learn to cope with alcohol at home, instead of experimenting while out driving with a group of other young people. That is not to say that drinking ought to be encouraged. But if the youngster insists on testing himself in this adult habit, let him do so under private family auspices and under propitious circumstances.

All these questions—the use of the car, smoking, drinking, dating, hours, use of the family phone— are essentially questions of discipline. Almost invariably, where parent and child have already passed through a lifetime of meaningful and reasonable rules and regulations, even the rambunctious and rebellious nature of the adolescent will not prevent him from striking a responsive chord. But for the parent who only now begins to "clamp down" when adolescence encroaches on family happiness and serenity, trouble may well be ahead.

As the youngster enters middle and late adolescence, discipline may become a particular problem. The youngster feels an increasing need to rebel, to be independent. Unless such matters of discipline are handled with a good deal of sensitivity, what may have started as small brush fires between the teen-ager and his parents can erupt into major warfare. I have seen a number of such war victims in my office who have reported complete standoffs in their negotiations with their adolescents. By now, they are viewed almost as enemy aliens.

Let it be said in fairness to many adolescents that too many parents still insist on "unconditional behavior," whether they express it thus or not. It has always seemed to me that some forms of family discipline are indeed negotiable, and ought to be freely discussed in family conference. The advanced teen-ager, literally thrust as he is into a state of rebellion, should not have discipline blindly imposed on him. It seldom works.

I have always advised parents to sit down with their youngsters and agree together on the rules and regulations which they feel must be imposed. If they let their youngsters participate in the making of these rules, they may also expect him to abide by them. If he does not abide by them, they then have every right to remove these privileges as punishment. If, for example, a daughter returns home from a date later than the agreed-upon time, parents can and should withdraw the dating privilege the following week. The fifteen- or sixteen-year-old youngster is old enough to know that privileges must be earned and that promises must be kept, and that these are freedoms enjoyed only by people of some maturity and judgment.

If there is one note of caution which many parents should observe, it is that the demands upon adolescents should never exceed those normally expected for their group. In other words, their demands as parents should in large measure be similar to the highest expectations by other parents of *their* children.

Often I ask parents with problems of adolescent discipline to answer these questions: Are they expecting too much of their youngster? Were their demands unreasonable from the beginning? Did their child only accept them because he was afraid not to? How do other parents in his class handle this problem? These and others usually prove suitable check points.

If, as sometimes happens, parents decide to introduce rules somewhat different from other parents', an explanation to their youngster as to why they feel so strongly about a certain rule will help him accept it much more easily. Parental discipline should never be determined by mass rule, even if such standards are passed and approved by the local PTA. Their best guide is their own judgment. I have known a number of highly responsible and mature parents who have insisted on standards of behavior for their youngsters far above those generally adhered to by their teen-age group. The parents' own example of behavior and conduct was so exemplary, I suspect that even a rebellious teen-ager found such conduct worthy of imitation. Perhaps, if we had more such "islands of propriety and excellence," the general disruptive tone of teen-age behavior could be considerably uplifted and improved.

Just as important to the middle and late adolescent as discipline and behavior is the whole question of sex. In the previous chapter I referred to the "pseudosexuality" of the early adolescent. By mid-adolescence, both boys and girls become sufficiently developed physically that both the excitement and the hazards of sex become powerful ingredients of life. For the teen-ager, the beauty of sex may lie in the spiritual power of love, while the hazards revolve about the fact that while nature provides the possibility of marriage at fifteen or sixteen, much of our society presses for a postponement by a number of years.

Sex drives differ markedly among normal adolescents. As we might expect, the boy's are considerably more overt than the girl's, and are much more easily stimulated. The girl's sexual drives are more easily controlled, and only really aroused after physical contacts. To put it another way, the boy is far more prone to express his sexual and physical desires freely. The normal girl, while feeling perhaps equally intense desires, finds it much easier to control her impulses and to steer a straight and level course.

Many people have the idea that the sex attitudes of today's teen-agers seem wholly determined by the standards of their own teen-age cult. While many of our older sex mores are certainly breaking down, sex attitudes of the individual middle and late adolescent are still strongly mirrored by his own childhood relations to his parents as well as by his parents' relationship to each other. This despite social strains continues to be true.

On the other hand, we can also observe all around us another kind of family pattern—of hate, of spite, infidelity, and selfishness—from which the adolescent draws clear conclusions. Such adolescents often regard the sex relationship as little more than animalistic. These patterns of life, too, can pass from one generation to the next. To that particular adolescent, all the blandishment and sermonizing that society might conjure up will seem little more than adult hypocrisy.

It is equally difficult to convince a young girl that most boys are honorable, gentle human beings, when she lives with a father who is dissolute and promiscuous. To those of us who have the daily opportunity to observe family patterns over a long period of time, it is amazing to find with what a high percentage of certainty we can perdict the future sexual attitudes of the child by looking at the child's parents as marriage partners, as well as the relationship between parent and child. We do know many youngsters who have successfully entered a marriage partnership in spite of earlier childhood patterns which clearly cast doubt on such success. But these are the exceptions, and not the rule. Unhappiness, more often than not, begets more unhappiness; abnormality begets abnormality; failure begets failure.

During the latter years of adolescence, there occurs also a number of inner anxieties that differ between boys and girls but play important roles for both in setting sexual behavior patterns. For the boy, these represent the twin anxieties of expressing his masculinity and his ability to win and keep the girl whom he may love. Some of the outlandish behavior of adolescent boys is clearly attributable to their need to impress their girl friends with their own prowess, boldness, and their competitive ability to do everything better than any other boy. The girl's anxieties, on the other hand, have more to do with her ability to attract the opposite sex. Once this has happened, will she be able to respond fully to a sexual relationship? With no past experience, her anxiety is as much based on this unknown factor as that inevitable moment when her womanly responses will be tested.

The increasing mobility of our teen-agers, the general relaxing of family ties, and effective contraceptive devices are unquestionably contributing to more and more premarital sex relationships. Appeals along the line of higher moral principles more often than not fall on deaf adolescent ears. What continues to make a good deal of difference in adolescent behavior and restraint is the kind of family life to which the youngsters have been exposed over the course of a lifetime. If parents have, through the years, provided this rich investment in ideals, in self-respect, and in a high regard for each other, these precepts will continue to act as a restraint, even during a period of high emotional stress and physical temptation.

To this vital question of adolescent sexuality many parents seek answers as to just what constitutes normal or abnormal adolescent behavior. This is difficult to answer, particularly at a time when social values are shifting in such broad areas of our culture. Excessive sexuality in young boys and girls can often be a sign of emotional disturbance. This is particularly true of the promiscuous adolescent girl, since overt sexuality in normal girls is far less prevalent than in boys.

Disturbed adolescents handle their individual sexuality in a variety of ways. We can have a little better understanding of what constitutes normal and abnormal teen-age sexual behavior by taking a closer look at some of the problems which occur.

A common type of sex-related disturbance is that of Joan. Joan is an eighteen-year-old girl who was referred to me because of extreme nervousness. She soon admitted to me that she was very much disturbed by the fact that her menstrual periods had stopped entirely. Several months of therapy passed before she was able to connect this event with the attraction she had developed toward a boy in her office. Joan approached a relationship with the boy with extreme caution. She was very much afraid of her own impulses. When her attraction to him took complete possession of her, she handled her fear by a total denial of her femininity.

Other adolescents, unlike Joan, deny their sexuality in a different fashion. Some make themselves utterly unattractive. This is particularly true of young people who are either extremely overweight or underweight. I recall treating a sixteen-year-old girl who was close to sixty pounds overweight. She tried one diet after another but, even after medical assistance, was unable to lose weight. Not until she was able to resolve her fear of sex could Ann successfully attack her serious weight problem and reduce to more attractive dimensions. There are many such Anns, all with similar problems.

Some youngsters become sexual delinquents. This is rarely a result of being oversexed, but rather an expression of a need to be loved on a dependent level. Edna P., a sixteen-year-old girl, was referred to me because of her promiscuity. As Edna had grown into adolescence, she increasingly felt the need to find someone who would love and protect her. She received no emotional support at home. If she could only relate sexually, she felt, she would be loved. So she flitted from boy to boy, none of whom had any genuine regard for her. Edna, of course, represents one of the most widespread examples of sexual disturbance, the endless and fruitless searcher for love and affection.

When we discuss adolescence, the lines between what we consider normal and abnormal are often difficult to draw. The intensity of adolescent problems will in large measure depend upon how the individual has solved all the previous problems of life, particularly in the areas of personal independence and sex.

The adolescent period represents a rocky road. Emotional breakdowns are frequent. The child's ego during these years remains underdeveloped. This holds for his superego as well. For even a normal fifteen-year-old boy the sexual drive may prove too strong and his ego still too weak to deal with strong impulses which he rightfully suspects may very well overwhelm him. Such anxieties can develop to a pitch where even professional psychotherapists find it difficult to discern a "normal" boy with "abnormal" problems from the truly neurotic adolescent.

A good example of typical adolescent behavior is a mechanism which we call "devaluation." We use the term to describe the way a child upon entering adolescence may mentally modify the power and infallibility of his parents, so that he himself may emerge more easily as an individual with his own capacity to make decisions. To achieve this young adolescents will often repudiate all that their parents have considered good and worthwhile. The important distinction is this: In the normal adolescent, the period of "devaluation" is a transient one. The status in which he holds his parents may decline momentarily. But in maturity there emerges a pattern of life which allows his parents' values to coexist alongside his own.

In the disturbed adolescent, however, this process of "devaluation" continues. The pendulum never swings back. The standards of the parents, the school, and the community become permanently devalued, and the child may easily end up as a juvenile delinquent. Such youngsters will often deliberately and repeatedly violate all normal rules of conduct as a part of their own disturbed need to establish their individuality.

Adolescent disturbance, of course, can strike anywhere, at any family, poor or wealthy, large or small, educated or uneducated, culturally endowed or undernourished. It can occur anywhere, and any time. Sometimes, disturbance appears to break out suddenly, but rarely is this true.

Fifteen-year-old Edward is a good example of a disturbed teen-ager, who from all outward appearances has had every advantage imaginable. Up to six months ago, Edward was an honor student in one of Westchester County's best private schools. But last week two desperate parents came to see me because suddenly, they said, "Edward's world seems to have caved in." He had begun to fail in school. He absolutely refused to work for his marks. He had become sullen, hostile, rebellious, and hatedly antagonistic, particularly toward his father, whom he belittled at every opportunity. He acted as though possessed with the urge to belittle everything his father represented—his profession, his friends, his abilities, his life values, and his very performance as a father. The parents, both successful professional people, had had high hopes for their boy. Now, Edward seemed bent to destroy indiscriminately all that had been so sedulously laid out for him.

Contrary to his parents' impression, however, Edward's trouble had begun a long time ago. After long and repeated interviews with both Edward and his parents, the mosaic of his personality emerged clearly. He had developed serious feeding problems at an early age, at which point his mother had pitted all her strength and ingenuity against his. He had adamantly refused food. For a time he had to be fed intravenously. His sister was born when he was six, and he had repeatedly attempted to harm her as a baby. Much of his life seems to have been dedicated to a bitter struggle between himself and his parents, directed particularly against his father. It was clear that because his parents placed unusual emphasis on education, he reacted by suddenly totally turning his back on his school responsibilities.

Edward now threatens to join that large group of one out of every ten teen-agers who drop out of school and make little further use of their intellectual abilities. In Edward's case a spiteful revenge against his parents may result in permanently destroying a very considerable human talent.

Adolescent rebellion against parental authority and values are often symptomatic of a disturbed personality. A variety of studies has clearly shown that one major cause of juvenile delinquency is the early stunting of emotional development. This can happen for a thousand reasons, but it is almost invariably the parent who is deeply involved. If any single major blame can be assessed in this whole dreary picture of adolescent disturbance and juvenile delinquency, the finger must point to the parent. This is precisely the reason why all parents should resolve to strengthen their role as a major influence on the younger generation. Parents must not only give of their love and their devotion, but they must also be prepared to respond to the changing needs of the time.

The rise in juvenile delinquency can only be partially attributed to broken homes and poverty. A recent United States Senate subcommittee reported that juvenile delinquency was increasing in suburban areas at an annual rate of seven percent. Richard B. Rogers, executive director of the Family Service Association of Nassau County, New York, speaks with authority on this point: "Case histories," he recently reported, "indicate a potential increase in juvenile delinquency in suburban areas among youngsters from white collar families. We are paying for the neglect of the past when we didn't have services available. The major proportion of adults bring their problems into marriage. We should have gotten to these parents when they were children. Unless we get to the average family, we are going to see more and more delinquency."

"Troubled teen-agers," says another report from another well-to-do community, "come from every type of home, but in common they share parental neglect." In short, much of today's delinquency began ten or fifteen years ago. Just how and when it began only parents can tell. Most of them apparently had insufficient insight to do anything about it. Based on a continuing study of several large adolescent groups, early childhood experiences emerge as crucial: According to Dr. Sheldon Glueck, about 90 percent of delinquents manifest some deviation from the norm before they are ten, and most of them by five or six.

Let me emphasize that it is not true that emotional childhood disturbance and juvenile delinquency are always the effect of some unfortunate family circumstance. In most cases the problem is blamed on an alcoholic father or a truant mother. In reality, of course, the cause and effect relationships of emotional disturbance operate far more subtly. The source of the problem goes much deeper.

Let me illustrate the point through two of my patients. Both are disturbed adolescents, but for quite different reasons. Andrew is a boy of superior intelligence, of exceptionally pleasant personality and charm. But Andrew is also a boy who is constantly getting into trouble. "It's almost as if Andy really wanted to get into hot water," his best friend told me. His friend showed excellent insight. Andrew functions poorly in school. He frequently fumbles the ball during football practice, even though he has proved himself a top athlete. He is extremely accident prone. He is constantly getting himself involved in a long series of misdeeds, after which he seems relieved at being caught.

What lay behind such odd behavior? Andrew's father had always been detached from the boy. He had turned to his mother for love, but she seemed to prefer his younger brother. Hostility toward both mother and brother developed, finally deepening into acute anger. For years he wished that his baby brother were dead. Soon he began to experience feelings of extreme guilt, and his adolescent behavior seemed to suggest a terrible scourge of self-punishment.

Our second boy is Donald. Donald did not get into the same difficulties as Andrew. He had suffered from learning and reading problems since he was young. Unlike Andrew, he related poorly to other boys, and his general insecurity was soon brought to the attention of his parents by his teachers. Remedial reading counseling in grammar school helped. But when he graduated to high school, he began to steal and quickly got himself into trouble with the authorities. What had happened to change him for the worse?

Donald's father had been away on business a good deal of the time. His mother felt quite unable to cope with running a household and managing a family for weeks on end. As a parent-figure she might as well have been away with his father. Donald felt rejected and insecure. He had no one from whom he could absorb strength. Soon, he gave in to his impulses and began to steal. He had convinced himself that he could never get these things at home from parents who did not seem to care. Neither his father nor mother was equipped to convince him differently.

The tragedy of such cases lies in the fact that so many of these heartaches could have been prevented with sufficient parental insight and understanding. Only too often, these come too little and too late. The hazards of serious emotional disturbance during adolescence are of course particularly acute. While the seeds of such disturbance usually go back many years, adolescence even under usual circumstances represents a period when the youngster will need every normal instinct and healthy emotion. The hazards of adolescence remain, but they are overcome. They subside and disappear with the approach of young adulthood. But in disturbed children, they persist and often multiply like a cancer. Then the emotional disturbance becomes a life sentence.

Parents are best advised never to sell their children short on love, affection, and devotion. The words come easily, but they represent a lifetime of labor of love. And when adolescence does arrive, remember these ten simple commandments:

1. Remind yourself often that every one of your children is a person unto him- or herself, that they live in different times with constantly shifting standards that may differ from those current when you were a child.

2. Excel in patience toward your teen-age youngster. Listen to him, but don't laugh at him. Don't force your advice down his throat, unless he is willing to listen.

3. Devote more time to encouraging the good in him, less time on punishing the bad.

4. Don't impose qualifications and conditions on your love.

5. Take a good look at yourself. Are you letting

your own emotional needs determine those of your children? Are you helping them in their drive for independence? Are you forcing something on them that compensates for something you yourself might have been missing?

6. When conflicts do arise, choose your times and battlegrounds wisely. Try to avoid such conflicts during bedtime, mealtime, weekends, or in public.

7. Do respect his desire for privacy and keep him informed of family matters.

8. Remember your teen-ager's extreme sensitivities. Be nice to his friends and make them welcome at home. Avoid sarcasm, and stay away from criticism in the presence of others.

9. Enforce discipline and sound rules, but don't insist on dotting the "i" for the sake of "principles." In other words, show some flexibility instead of rigidity.

10. Look ahead and remember that these adolescent difficulties will be memories a few years hence.

1 "Social Influence on Adolescent Behavior," *Journal of the American Medical Association*, Vol. 182, No. 6, p. 644.

2 One of the major problems high school administrators have to deal with these days is where to park students' cars. Professor James Coleman, one of our most prominent authorities on adolescent behavior, recently found that in one school, 68 percent of all high school students owned their own cars by the spring of their senior year.

IX

The Silent Troubles

"THE CHILD'S SOB in the silence curses deeper than the strong man in his wrath," wrote Elizabeth Barrett Browning in *The Cry of Children*. Children who suffer silently suffer just as deeply as those who cry out. And because their suffering is silent, it is just that much more difficult for a parent to help. The child who turns inward is trying to solve his problems by running away from them. It is not a very good way, but perhaps the only way he knows.

Parents, even sensitive and well-meaning parents, often fail to reach the silent child, to find the root of the problem, however hard they try. It may be of course that the child is essentially shy by nature. But a shy child may also be retreating from the world, because he does not like what he sees and feels. That child has problems.

Sometimes, children with deep silent troubles end up in disaster. Some years ago, newspaper headlines carried the news of twenty-one-year-old post-debutante Suzanne Clift's murder of her lover, Pietro Brentani, a Swiss-Italian engineer. Suzanne was not born a murderess. Suzanne's background tells a classic history of parental neglect and deprivation. Her psychiatrist reported her to be suffering from "deprivation, depression, and hopelessness; masochistic with a capacity for satisfaction from suffering." Suzanne, according to all reports, had never known anything except rejection—as a baby, a young girl, and a young woman. Clearly she had grown out of touch with reality.

Children with problems have two ways to solve them: Either they act aggressively, which may include delinquency, or they can retreat into a shell in which they somehow feel safe. I often say to parents that such problem children have a basic choice: Fight or Flight. Aggression or Passivity.

Let us look at the child in flight. The aggressive child can never be ignored by his parents. The child in flight, however, is often overlooked by his parents since his silence cannot speak for him. The child in flight is a child of many ages. His appearance is not as unfamiliar as you might suspect. He is the little boy who cries in his crib upon the approach of an unfamiliar face; she is the sixteen-year-old high school junior too fearful to go to her first high school prom. The reasons why parents worry about their shy, silent children are frequently social rather than clinical. Few things hurt parents more than their child's inability to attract and hold friends. Some children are shy simply because they are socially awkward, and they usually get over this phase. But shy children with serious emotional problems do not desire friends, and even if they do, they are afraid of approaching them for fear of being rejected.

Parents in such cases frequently find all their encouragements to sociability of no avail. The teacher is their most valuable ally in bringing to their attention some possible emotional warning signs. Such disturbed children, who are often bright and intellectually gifted, frequently perform at less than satisfactory levels. The good teacher will soon distinguish the failings of the disturbed child from her slower but normal class-mate.

Typical of the shy and silent child is Marie, a pretty blue-eyed eight-year-old girl, whom I have been seeing for some time. Her teacher described her as well behaved, but extremely quiet, with-drawn, who "somehow seems frightened of some-thing."

Almost immediately, the initial therapy sessions began to bear out the teacher's impressions. Not a single word passed Marie's lips during the first two sessions. She appeared extremely cautious as she explored the playroom, taking care to touch nothing for fear of making a noise. In the third session the ice finally broke. In barely audible whispers, she performed a scene which is always an eye-opener to the therapist. Sitting in front of a large dollhouse which we use for play therapy, she began to portray the father doll as a highly punitive man, who seemed totally tyrannical to-ward his wife and daughter. The mother, as Marie played it, was as frightened of the man as the daughter, which further reinforced the child's own fears. Using these dolls, she played out her family drama.

The girl's play proved revealing. It was appar-ent that if we could somehow help the father to be less of a tyrant and more of an understanding fa-ther, at least some of Marie's emotional handicaps might be eliminated. Now at our clinic we see both Marie's father and mother in separate ses-sions. Progress is being made. Marie's father turned out indeed to be a tyrant, while her mother proved most infantile and totally submissive to her husband's every wish. All of Marie's life was oriented around the goal of "keeping Daddy happy and not angry." Difficult as it may be for him to realize, he now sees that the damage already done to his daughter's emotional makeup is almost entirely due to his behavior.

Who could blame Marie for withdrawing into her own little shell, in which she could fashion her own safe destiny and happiness? We must remember that the withdrawn and anxious child rarely can react positively to a given situation. She simply cannot face up to it. Unfortunately, what may initially be a temporary expediency may turn into a habitual way of life. A neurosis is a way of life, and so is schizophrenia, but both are controllable some of the time, if caught and treated at an early stage. We are now quite certain that Marie will grow up to be a normal and well-adjusted person.

Withdrawing from life rarely accomplishes anything. But most of us have long been adults before life's experience teaches us this lesson. Such insights cannot be expected of the young child. He can only live by instinct. Instinct will often tell a child that he fares best by ducking an issue, by escaping notice, because only in this way, he feels, is he out of danger. Then he can avoid conflict with the powers which necessarily circumscribe his life —his parents, his teachers, his older brothers and sisters.

All of us in child therapy observe many anxiety-ridden silent children, who have become what they are not because of an abnormal family existence, such as Marie's, but in spite of what we would consider relatively normal family relationships. Can chidren make mountains out of molehills? They can very easily, especially if the molehills are real enough and they are encountered once too often. In a child's vivid mind, a hundred minor adult rejections may build up into what he is convinced is total rejection and the unloving treatment of a busy mother may eventually translate itself in the little mind into total abandonment and a dark world of rejection.

Let us look at what might be called a "typical" boy, Johnny, who seems to be absolutely normal. But he has a father too busy with his own life to pay much attention to him, and a mother too harassed by life's challenges to be sensitive to her child's problems. Johnny also has five brothers and sisters, all vying for attention.

This is all quite normal. But today, Johnny is not absolutely normal. He is not even home. He is in an institution for emotionally ill children. His recovery will be slow and painful, and will be counted in years, not months.

How could this happen? Johnny's life started out well enough, but when his brothers and sisters came along, he felt he was being gradually edged out by his parents' increasing concern with the younger children. As so often happens with emotional actions and reactions, feelings began to build up. They came to be irrational and quite uncontrollable. Johnny's conviction that his brothers and sisters received all of his parents' attention made him violently angry. As a device to create more attention for himself, he behaved so deplorably that the situation was only aggravated. His behavior resulted in further rejection and isolation, with punishment following punishment. He felt increasingly less wanted and less loved. His daily existence became unbearable, punctuated by scenes, parental reprimands, then further punishment.

Since Johnny could not solve his family's problems, he solved them for himself in the only way he knew. He totally rejected his parents and retreated into his own world of fantasy, in which he was loved and fully accepted. He entered the world of the schizophrenic. He soon lost all contact with reality, relying solely on the word he himself had created. Many years of therapy will be needed to draw Johnny back into the real world. In the meantime, we must attempt to change Johnny's real and outer world as well, so that Johnny will become convinced that here is a world worth returning to. But for the next few years, Johnny will spend his time in a special boarding school staffed with trained personnel who can help him retrace his steps into reality. Johnny's case fortunately is not typical. But there are enough children like him to make this a tragic story of early emotional deprivations resulting in an acutely unhappy life, which will haunt the memories of these children and their families for the rest of their days.

There are in the annals of medicine some remarkable cases where a youngster's withdrawal into himself, a return to the womb, has literally produced physical deformities. Recently, thirty-seven-year-old Wisconsin man underwent three hours of surgery to lengthen the tendons at his hips and knees which had shrunk from long misuse. "The spasms that had bundled him into helplessness 22 years before," reported *Time* magazine, "were his unconscious solution to the shock of being removed from his mother's protectiveness. They were the closest he could come to a 'return to the womb,' and guaranteed him against ever again being expelled."

Physical crippling under these circumstances is a rarity. Emotional crippling, however, is common. How does it happen, and why? It is best to ask the question in anticipation of such emotional difficulties, rather than in the aftermath of emotional illness.

It is never easy to put one's finger on any one trauma or any single cause. But remember that as the child grows through his infancy into adolescence and beyond, he meets with a series of frustractions and challenges as a normal matter of course. The very process of growing up almost assures a necessary series of ordinary aches and pains, which serve as guidelines for the direction of the young life. But sometimes things interfere, which makes these normal aches and pains less tolerable or even insupportable. We sometimes observe a child whose ego is too weak to carry him through the shoals and eddies of a child's existence, which most children pass through without even a hint of difficulty.

Other children have a difficult beginning, a difficult birth, or some other experience so early in life that one wonders how it can be possibly permanently engraved on the child's memory. But it is. Sometimes, we know, it is due to the parents' own personal problems, which inevitably reflect on their youngsters. It could be their inability to tolerate behavior in their children which they interpret as being aggressive or sexual in nature. This may set up a whole set of interesting dynamics: If the parent rejects the behavior of the child, the child's own ego soon begins to reject it as well. Then often follows a struggle between his own urges and what his ego now tells him to be right and proper. He now internalizes the conflict between what his parents consider bad and his own needs as a human being. Now he whispers "no," "shame," or "bad" to himself, as he tries to control and repress urges which he tells himself are undesirable.

Sometimes these urges are not too well repressed, and they break through. This often results in an anxious child who is aware of harboring certain fears without actually knowing their cause. The anxious child is less afraid of external attack than he is of his struggle from within.

The life on the anxious child is not an easy one. He feels guilty, yet he often does not know why. He feels inadequate, and he fears to test his own adequacy, because he is afraid of failure, of being laughed at. He withdraws, his only possible response. He also retreats in his work at school, from sports activity and play, and from the closeness of his family. Trying out new experiences, meeting new people, all become major efforts. His time is taken up by longing desperately to please, never sure how other people feel about him and always afraid to find out.

The anxious child sits on the sidelines of life. Watching from the bleachers, he does not involve himself, but rather observes from a safe distance. He is also apt to punish himself. He will hurt himself rather than others, and he is quick to shoulder blame on himself. His aggressions, as we see, have been turned upon himself.

The anxious child, in short, is a bother to himself, rather than to anyone else. But while he is often quite literally a self-imposed social outcast, a surprisingly large number of such children carry on the surface sociabilities, preventing even parents from seeing through to the true state of affairs. As a matter of fact, the typically anxious child is often so "good" a child at home that his parents hardly know that he is around. Frequently, a mother of an anxious silent child will insist, "he is such a *good* child!" When we explain that surface behavior may obscure the real problem, parents are very surprised. Too much "goodness," therefore, may be suspect under certain circumstances. Alert and sensitive parents will watch most carefully to ensure that such "goodness" may not be in fact an emotional means of escaping involvement.

Such "good" children often have some experience in their history which obliges them to be good, if they are to be at all accepted. Looking into their past, we often find that such children's occasional badness—common to all children—was not accepted, and that such parental nonacceptance became an unbearable burden for the child.

The anxious child may develop other serious symptoms, which can seriously affect the use of his mind. Such children often sense that love will only be forthcoming as long as they comply totally with the thoughts and wishes of others. Their mental processes therefore begin to atrophy to the point where they rely wholly on the thinking of others.

Lucy was such a girl. Thirteen years old, she was referred to me because she appeared depressed. She was unable to make friends and seemed withdrawn and subdued. To observe Lucy in school, you would guess her to be below average in performance and intelligence. Tests, however, showed her to have an I.Q. of 130, far above average. But her brightness fell on fallow ground. Lucy did well on "Yes" and "No" quizzes, but she totally blocked on any test which called for individual thinking and the expression of ideas. Lucy cut a pitiful figure in class, creating considerable sympathy among her classmates. Yet, she invariably would withdraw from their friendly approaches.

Who is Lucy, and why should such a gifted child

be such a failure? To find part of the answer, we will first have to look at her family. Lucy is much the youngest of four children, born to parents already in their late forties. She was unplanned, and, as the parents frankly admitted "an accident." Because of the wide age gaps, Lucy was a social outcast among her older brothers and sisters, as well as her parents, who were totally unprepared to take on another baby at their age. Lucy's father is a prominent scientist. He makes up in intellect for what he lacks in compassion and feelings. So far as Lucy was concerned, her father gave her all of the necessary material things, but supplied none of her emotional needs. The only way for her to satisfy his demands was to attempt to live the life of perfection which he demanded of all his children. The mother, a plain, simple woman, was no factor in the relationship. She stood totally in her husband's shadow.

Lucy's school performance deteriorated. Her lack of self-confidence sharply contrasted with an unusually gifted father. She naturally felt that her poor schoolwork fitted the pattern of her imagined inferiority. Her father frequently called her "stupid," asking for scholastic accomplishment quite above what could be expected at Lucy's age level.

As I have already mentioned, such children rarely blame their external environment. Lucy blamed herself, not her father. She regarded him as a good father in his attempts to help her. But her own ego had been sat upon for so long that she was unable to rise above it.

Lucy's continued failures in school finally prompted her father to seek psychiatric help. Many months of intensive therapy with Lucy as well as her father gradually created the kind of tolerable family condition which made Lucy use the many abilities which she had always possessed. Lucy's father came to realize that he could not judge her in his own image, but that he must regard her as a person in her own right.

Lucy's own therapy proved slow and arduous. We used every possible opportunity to nurture her badly damaged ego. She soon developed new skills and talents, and constant praise and encouragement drove her on to an increased self-confidence. It also allowed her to involve herself again with other people in a variety of social activities.

I think Lucy's case is particularly interesting, since it provides us with an illustration of the fact that even the most intelligent of parents can induce in their children the saddest of all emotional states. One is tempted to add that they do so unknowingly, but I cannot give the parents the benefit of the doubt when even a flicker of insight into the child's world would easily throw much-needed light onto the darkened corners of a parent-child relationship.

To the child, as well as the parent, value-systems are not always what they appear to be. Lucy's father thought he was being a good father by expecting of his daughter a level of performance which he assumed would fit a thirteen-year-old girl as well as a brilliant scientist in his fifties. He was not as good a father as he imagined.

Another common confusion of values has to do with parental concepts of ideal child behavior which at times become impossible burdens to the child. Not long ago, a much-frustrated mother brought in her six-year-old boy. Jimmy, she told me, was desperately frightened of other children. They called him a "sissie," and he would run away from a fight or any threat of violence. How could this possibly be, she asked?

A few weeks of therapy and interviews gave us at least a partial answer: The mother's own problems seemed to be the core of the difficulty. She was terrified of her own hostility and could not tolerate it in her child. This, incidentally, is quite a common behavior pattern in both men and women, and only rarely recognized by even their closest and most prescient friends. Jimmy's mother presented a façade of sweetness and flexibility to the outside world, which served to hide her real feelings. This masquerade was a fulltime job for her, and it took its own toll. Her armor of sweetness failed to be punctured, even when I purposefully pricked it at one of her more vulnerable emotional spots. She told me that it was far better to "turn the other cheek" than to retaliate. When Jimmy was two years old he had begun to show some of the normal aggressiveness of a growing young boy. His overt behavior apparently awakened all kinds of anxiety feelings in his mother. She simply could not tolerate it for her own peace of mind. Aggression is bad in any form, she told Jimmy, and was not to be permitted. This denial of aggressive feelings came to be part of Jimmy's own makeup, and he soon equated passivity with goodness and proper behavior. The final test for him came with the advent of school. He was simply unable to cope with the task of living with thirty other lively youngsters. In defense, he immediately withdrew into what he considered the normal behavior patterns of his totally passive home environment.

Therapy followed. Jimmy's mother was helped to recognize that limited aggressiveness is a perfectly normal expression of the personality, and that it is not necessarily bad. Jimmy, she further recognized, had to be given ample opportunity to develop his own character and outlets in every possible normal way.

Jimmy, in separate sessions, slowly accepted the fact that all forms of self-expression are not necessarily bad. All children, he soon came to know, bear some anger and even hatred toward others, and that this side of life is known and perfectly acceptable. Jimmy soon grew freer in his therapy, for awhile even swinging to the opposite extreme and expressing overt aggressions as if making up for lost time. Soon he came to control himself, and his emotional gyroscope began to function normally.

I use the term "emotional gyroscope' 'to make an important point. While a gyroscope helps to stabilize a ship in heavy seas, it does not prevent a reasonable amount of response to the surface of the sea. So it is with emotions. Even with the best emotional balance, we must expect and accept wide individual differences. A child may be perfectly normal and still be shy. Any child indeed may have real cause to be anxious, and still remain a perfectly well-adjusted human being. We sometimes see mothers who wonder whether shyness in their children stems from an emotional cause, when it is in fact only a minor social handicap, if that.

Fathers feel particularly strongly about this matter of shyness. They keep a sharp eye on their children who may exhibit marked degrees of shyness or social awkwardness. Our society places such premium on channeled aggression as part of the success of living, that the lack of it is felt by many to be a social handicap of considerable consequence. "Life's a jungle," one such father pontificated recently, "and my boy's got to scrap and fight just like the rest of us."

But nature is hard to change. Some children by nature are more recessive and more quiet than others. There is nothing wrong with them. We need them as much as the extrovert. Introspective children frequently turn out to be creative and grow into refreshingly independent thinkers.

Parents must also view their children's fears in proper balance. Even normal children harbor fears of some kind or another. Often, they are parent-inspired. I have run across a number of children who became terribly frightened by thunderstorms, especially when these occurred at night. Curiously enough, I discovered that when they were small, these children used to sleep soundly enough through the most violent thunderstorms. It was not until their parents began picking them up in anticipation of such fears that they became aware that there was anything to be frightened about.

Fears among perfectly normal children may be far more common than most of us realize. In a recent survey of 482 children in Buffalo, New York, exactly one-half admitted to suffering from "honest-to-goodness" fears. Foremost on their list were fears of using other people's glasses, dishes, silver, and towels. Fear of snakes was also high on the list. So also were fears of death and accidents, thunder and lightning, cuts and bruises, school marks, blood, bugs, darkness, and other assorted terrors.

Another recent survey pointed to the disquieting fact that half of our youngsters live in dread of a nuclear attack. They worry about being poisoned by fallout, of being separated from their parents, about injury or death to their families and themselves. These are new but real fears, in large part reflections of the only partly expressed fears of their elders.

"To the degree that we adults become fearful and suspicious," Dr. Benjamin Spock recently wrote, "we pass such attitudes on to our children. Specific studies have shown that when children are taught to fear others, it is always harmful to their personalities. Informed parents no longer try to control a youngster with threats of the bogeyman."

While I do not want to overemphasize the effect of possible nuclear attack on the emotional stability of the child, we should keep in mind that the child regards his parents as omnipotent. It comes as a shock, therefore, when he is told that the things that go on in Southeast Asia, in Cuba, or Moscow are events over which his parents have no control. It is better, it seems to me, to keep family discussions of outside threats to factual minimums, and if necessary, even impose some control over the child's TV programs and outside reading material which often enough bear on such worldwide subjects of violence.

For the *normal* child, these and the hundreds of other possible fears are very real, but they do not cripple. The parent can do much to help solve the child's normal set of fears and anxieties, and to keep him from withdrawing from life and developing what we have called the "silent troubles." We have already discussed the hidden hazards of an absolutely "good" child, as the term is used by some people.

Normal deviations of aggressiveness and naughtiness are healthy outlets for any child. We should accept the normal forms of hostility for what they are—individual means of expressing their own little problems. They only grow large if such emotional outlets are totally blocked.

I am not suggesting invariable parental acceptance of intolerable behavior. Nothing of the kind. But do look and try to see what is behind your child's behavior. Try to discover the cause rather than handle the symptom. Let me illustrate: If your nine- or ten-year-old child sucks more and more, you will naturally grow increasingly annoyed and perhaps disgusted. The immediate temptation is to criticize his behavior and take all measures to prevent its recurrence. Instead, it would be better to try to see what might lie behind it all. What is so lacking in the child's world, you might ask yourself, that makes a nine-year-old regress to an earlier stage of life? Scolding and punishment may not only terminate the sucking, but may in fact increase its frequency because of added frustration.

We have explored a number of ways in which children retreat from a life situation which they feel they can neither face nor conquer. Even the most normal child likes to retreat once in a while. Children who play house or hide under their blankets for fun enjoy a temporary retreat into something which is warm and more secure than acceptance of the challenges outside.

While children withdraw from life to varying degrees, total withdrawal may frequently connote childhood schizophrenia, one of the most serious of mental illnesses. We still know comparatively little about the exact causes of schizophrenia. Throughout the country, an estimated half million youngsters are thought to be clearly schizophrenic, or borderline cases. One out of every four mental hospital patients in the country is a schizophrenic.

Treatment is exceedingly slow, and progress is measured at a snail's pace.

Childhood schizophrenics have totally withdrawn from life. Sometimes, symptoms become apparent in the first few months of life, although onset at ages one through three are much more common. But although much schizophrenia begins then, many cases are not discovered until adolescence and beyond. Symptoms vary, and include many of the withdrawal patterns we have already discussed. Other symptoms abound as-well: odd speech effects, repetitous play patterns and absorption in fantasy. I have seen schizophrenic children who laugh wildly and scream like animals. Some remain mute for years or become violent biters, scratchers, or kickers. One of the tragedies of the disease is the fact that several years may pass between the time the parents notice some odd behavior and the time they become sufficiently alarmed to do something about it. "Just as cancer must be treated early to secure a reasonable chance of success," warn two experts in the field, "so childhood schizophrenics should be treated as early as possible. Certainly part of the reason for the present poor prognosis of this condition is due to the delay in onset of therapy."

While no one expects a parent to make a diagnosis, people trained in child psychiatry can. The child who feels that the only way that he can deal with his conflicts is to retreat completely from life is potentially a seriously ill child. It is the extent and degree of totality of withdrawal which are the telling signs. In the later stages of advanced schizophrenia, it would be difficult indeed to ignore the symptoms. Here is how a mother of a nine-year-old schizophrenic child described her daughter, who had totally withdrawn into an unreal world of her own: Mary was only two years old when her mother went to the hospital to have her third child. "While at her aunt's," the mother reminisced, "she began to spend time rocking back and forth on the floor. She became afraid of cars and of being left alone. Feeding and sleeping problems followed. When it was brought to our pediatrician's attention he said to bring her home immediately, which we did. Following this, she had a bladder infection which was treated with shots for over a year. Mary became intensely afraid of the doctor during this time and began to be afraid of any man, including her father. She would go screaming through the house, shutting all doors as she went, until she was in the farthest closet. There she would be found, sitting and rocking on the floor.

"Our pediatrician failed to recognize these symptoms at this time, saying that I was an over-anxious mother and Mary was a spoiled child. Her fears continued to grow and her cries became sharper and her screaming more intense until August, when the doctor suggested putting her in nursery school to break up what he called 'the strong mother-daughter tie.' This we did in a nursery school one block away. She seemed to enjoy the first half-hour or so, but when I left to go home she started screaming hysterically. I took her home in a state of shock, and every time I moved her in my arms she clung to me and started to scream. Mucus ran from her mouth and she had a lost, wild look. Mary regressed very rapidly from this point, almost into infancy. She slept in a fetal position and the sitting and screaming became much worse, with poor appetite, little sleep, and rocking during the night.

"I was frantic and, receiving no help from my

pediatrician, contacted another friend who sent me to her doctor. He referred us to another pediatrician, who sedated her and sent her to a psychologist. He tested Mary and diagnosed her as having 'brain damage.' At this point Mary's fear of the car, noises, and vigrations was so great that when we took her to the psychologist she was stiff in my arms, almost unconscious. Many varied diagnoses and treatment approaches followed. It was not until she entered the hospital at the age of seven years that we finally realized she was suffering from childhood schizophrenia."[1]

If this spells out a rather frightening picture of a family in agony, it is. Still, there is hope. Progress is slowly being made, even in this most difficult area. When diagnosed early enough, 60 or 75 percent of such cases can be salvaged. They are worth saving, both in the human terms of the individual and in the contribution to society which is otherwise lost. Dr. Leo Kanner, often called the dean of child psychiatry, recalls a schozophrenic boy whom he treated successfully. The boy, in his words, grew up to be an "oddball," but an outstanding scientist. Nonetheless, we recognize that the level of psychiatric knowledge about various forms of schizophrenia is as yet fragmental and experimental at best. We do not yet know whether the causes of schizophrenia are entirely emotional or physical. We suspect a combination of both.

To the parents of such a child, the question of schizophrenic causation is of little import, compared to whether or not their child will once again lead a normal and happy life. We know that for the withdrawn child, time that elapses without help only increases the burden, the hopelessness, and the tears. The child who is withdrawn, who turns within himself, is not much different from any normal child. All sensitive human beings withdraw a little when they are hurt. But we withdraw momentarily. The silent child's reaction is not as elastic. He is hurt more deeply, and withdraws still further without coming back. Parents, more than anyone else, can help him come back. It takes a bridge to love and understanding, to help lead the child from his nightmarish world of fantasy to the real world of Belonging. To belong somewhere is all they want.

It is little enough to ask.

1 *Journal of the American Medical Association*, Vol. 171, No. 8, October 24, 1959, p. 1,046.

X

The Aggressive Child

CHILDREN, JUST AS ADULTS, face anxieties in one of two ways. As discussed in the previous chapter, many children attempt to solve their anxieties by total or partial withdrawal. Problems are not faced but evaded by a variety of defense mechanisms. Often, as we have seen, seemingly insoluble problems become supplanted in the child's mind by flights of unreality, which fit more comfortably his emotional scheme of things. He withdraws.

The aggressive child, on the other hand, exhibits entirely different behavior problems, requiring very different parental handling, and professional treatment when indicated.

There are certain general observations to be made about the aggressive child. He is, first of all, in far greater evidence than the withdrawn child. Aggressive children do not necessarily outnumber their withdrawn counterparts. They are, however, more visible, more easily detectable, potentially more dangerous to society, and for all of these reasons more likely to receive clinical attention.

Aggressive children, unlike their withdrawn counterparts, can become acute behavior problems. These can range from mild manifestations of stubbornness, temper tantrums, or soiling, to the extremes of killing, arson, and mayhem.

Each type of aggression will be gone into here, since many parents find it particularly difficult to handle their aggressive child in ways which may effectively control their anger and anxiety without extinguishing the spirit to live and to compete in a healthy way. The difficulty stems from several sources. The most obvious is the simple fact that we live today in a world in which aggression is variously celebrated and lamented, where some forms of social and vocational aggressions are perfectly accepted, but which in our private lives may be frowned upon. A boy may become seriously confused when he views his father's aggressive business success at the same time he is told that he must not compete too aggressively with his own brothers and sisters.

There are, therefore, so far as the child is concerned, vaguely delineated value judgments to be made about aggressive behavior in general, and more specifically about "good" and "bad" kinds of aggression. Can he tell the difference? He looks at television. There some kind of aggression forms the basic ingredient of most dramatic plots. The Western, the war films, murder, cops-and-robbers, and international spies parade before him, little life vignettes, which may not always be portrayed as wholesome, but always as exciting and stimulating.

Most children, fortunately, can distinguish between the world of make-believe and the real world. There is no doubt in my mind, however, that our society does everything possible to convince the child who has difficulty in making such distinctions that aggressive behavior pays off.

While I am certain that most people are not at all committed to the cause of aggressive behavior, too many, I fear, are excessively tolerant or minor aggressions. Our mental health clinics and our criminal and juvenile courts are filled with hundreds of thousands of young men and women, who once transgressed "harmlessly," but then let their aggressions get out of hand. Many of these transgressing adolescents and adults were once boys and girls, pulling dogs' tails, heaving pop bottles into neighbors' windows, or binding a playmate to a tree in Indian style.

There was once a sixteen-year-old boy by the name of Charles Whitman, who could plug a squirrel in the eye with his gun better than anyone else in his school. He "seemed to be oozing with hostility," reported a psychiatrist. Nine years later, that boy had turned his anger not on squirrels, but on human beings, killing thirteen and wounding thirty-one others during a lunch hour at the University of Texas.

Charles Whitman was an out and out psychotic, but the difference between him and the neurotically aggressive child and the juvenile delinquent is only a matter of degree. Common to all is an expressed hostility toward other people and often toward themselves. The broad extent of childhood aggression is perhaps better seen by a recent study of New York City's school children. Almost one-half of the nearly one million school children in the system were felt to require some kind of individual help, a predominant number showing some form of aggressive behavior problem.

What kind of help can be given such children, and how can we help them solve their problems? Clinics such as my own cannot possibly cope with all of the children with aggressive behavior problems whose parents now seek our help. Of those we do see, a great many can be helped to channel their aggressions in creative ways. Others are not so lucky. They have progressed so far that treatment either comes too late or proves ineffective. From my own experience, such serious cases seem to come with increasing frequency. Here is a typical example out of my case file:

John P., age nine. Referred to Clinic because of destruction of property. Set fire to neighbor's garage year ago. History of breaking into property and destruction. School performance poor, first grade repeated. John is oldest of seven children. Four brothers, two sisters. Mother expecting eighth child. Anamnesis[1] shows marked depression and deprivation both physically and emotionally. Although John is only nine, he has six younger brothers and sisters, representing an almost annual displacement and progressive detachment and exclusion with apparently no understanding by his parents. John's conflicts, which involve retaliation against his brothers and sisters and parents, seem to have been released indiscriminately on the community by his anti-social conduct.

The boy has since been sent to a state hospital. Therapy proved ineffective, and there was no choice but to have him committed to a public institution.

Most cases of aggressive behavior problems do not end this sadly. Indeed, the large majority of aggressive children can be helped, as long as parents read the symptoms early enough and take appropriate action.

Typical of an early aggressive behavior problem is the case of three-year-old Tommy, who destroyed every toy he ever possessed. His toys' life expectancy, his mother assured me, ran something slightly over half an hour. Sometimes his destructive impulses would get out of hand, but his anger was invariably confined to his toys.

Toward his parents, Tommy remained a considerate and loving child.

We discovered quite quickly during play therapy what probably caused his seemingly inexplicable behavior. During his early training period, his parents had been extremely rigid, punitive, and demanding. They had never allowed him to show any negative or hostile feelings toward them. His utterly destructive drives toward inanimate things proved to be an outlet for his hostility, which he was not allowed to show toward his parents.

Tommy was quite easily helped to get over his feelings of hostility. His parents had sufficient insight to cooperate. But even where no unusual family circumstance like Tommy's exists, aggressions, fears, and anxieties may all be a natural part of growing up. A number of psychological studies have shown that the average child is not only aggressive by nature, but that he lives in continuous fear of being destroyed by the aggressions of the adult, in most cases the parent, who, after all, is much stronger and thus more dangerous in the child's view.

At the same time, the child also expects protection from the parent against all outside hostile influences. A child's security includes the parent's provisions for food, support, clothing, and love. When any of these needs are not met, the child may easily regard such parental oversight as a distinct deprivation. These children often interpret such deprivation as a form of adult aggression clearly directed against them. They may in turn strike back. This counter-aggression is frequently observed in children; yet in only relatively few cases does the parent think of himself as being in any way the cause.

I often talk to parents in these terms, to try to

help them see just why their children behave as they do. Their reaction is to tell me that everything I have told them sounds implausible and illogical. But this, I try to point out to them, is the child's view—plausible or implausible, logical or illogical—and these are the emotions which can trigger many of the childhood aggressions which we come later to lament.

It is difficult to view important childhood aggressions through the eyes of the child. Nonetheless, it is important that at least we try. These aggressions tend to operate on a far more primitive level than those of adults. To judge these aggressions on the pattern of adult experience is to miss the point entirely. Psychotherapists sooner or later come across the youngster who threatens "to kill" his parents, teacher, brothers, or sisters. A child's wish "to kill," however, is not to be taken literally, although such childish expressions can be a chilling prospect to the startled adult. The child's meaning of "kill" is merely a wish to remove that particular person from his sphere of life.

Why do children act aggressively, and why do they say they wish to "kill"? No definitive answer to that question is possible, at least as yet. The Freudian concept of aggression as a basic reaction to frustration, and as an instinctual drive to be equated with the death wish, does not seem to me the final explanation. Childhood aggressions are positive emotional responses to the very process of growing up. In the world of nature, survival would be less absurd without some forms of tacit outward behavior. Insects employ their antennae to grope for food as well as to avoid obstructions. They learn about their environment by such outward thrusts. The child, too, increasingly probes the dimensions of his own world. He can only do so by some similar outward act. Relating himself to the world about him, the child flexes his mind and heart by trial and error. These repeated probings will tell him how deep, how long, and how vigorously he may be able to explore and advance.

Some parents are apt to be critical of their child's aggressions in any form, however mild and harmless. Remember that for the child it is easier to be destructive than constructive; easier to be messy than neat; careless, instead of careful. Some parents manage to convince themselves that children who consistently leave their rooms in utter disarray must surely be doing so because of some hostility. In almost every case, this of course is not the case; rather it is an instance of simple carelessness.

One of the key observations to be made about childhood aggressiveness is not the attitude of the child, but rather the attitude of the parent. How do parents look at the act of aggression, at the consequences of aggressive behavior, and at the possible penalties of aggression? These are central questions. They are not easy to answer.

Many of us are inwardly confused as to whether we should welcome aggression or reject it. I think we all know why. In our modern society, we are torn between the virtues and dangers of aggressive behavior. Many people in their business and public life are compelled to behave aggressively, while the morality of family "togetherness" compels them to suppress these same aggressions at home.

Such disparate interpretations of aggression can be seen in our clinics as well, and the individual's reaction to aggression is frequently part of the clinical picture. I can readily illustrate the point by citing two of my patients: One of them is a highly successful business executive. His wife described him to me proudly as a "real aggressive go-getter." Having observed him at close hand, it was my impression that this man did not let grass grow under his feet. Another wife also described her husband as aggressive. But she thought of aggression as "pushy" or "brutish." The relationship rests on a pretty precarious foundation.

Our attitudes to aggression deserve some self-examination. Once having done so, we can better judge the aggressive nature of our children. Let us make some further general observations about aggression. Aggression can be turned inward or outward. In its most extreme illustrations murder is the ultimate act of outward aggression, suicide the ultimate inward aggressive act. It is the outward form of aggression which is most easily discernible, and it is this form which I want to discuss now. There are many people who would like to act out their aggressions, but are held back for fear of disapproval, discovery, or ridicule. As a result they literally "eat their hearts out," turning all of their aggressive acts inward.

Aggression carries other faces as well. We can express it directly, or we can turn it onto someone who only rarely is immediately involved. Innocent bystanders are often hit. If we are furious with our boss in the office, we are not apt to express it directly for fear of risking our jobs, but we will probably take it out on our husband or wife, a fellow worker, our secretary, the bus driver, or whoever happens to be in the way.

Quite often, as a matter of fact, aggression begets aggression. One man's frustration becomes another man's aggression, and it can thus cultivate and repeat itself over and over again.

Could we build a world for our children in which

frustrations and all confrontations would be eliminated? We could not. Even if we could, it would
be a grave mistake to attempt it. We could no
more picture our world without frustrations than
the Wonderful World of Oz without its series of
individual challenges. It would be difficult to see
how a child could sharpen his own personality
without the abrasive encounters of occasional frustrations and difficulties. Were we to eradicate
frustration from the life of the youngster, the
majority of our college freshmen would still be
sucking their milk bottles.

If an adult needs an excuse to act aggressively,
the child needs none. He is told to stop sucking his
thumb, to discard his milk bottle, to stop wetting
his diapers, to stop masturbating, to stop cuddling
his mother because it is time to go to school, to sit
still, to be quiet, to say something, to be nice to
Uncle, when of course it would be much more fun
to pull his sister's pigtails.

Frustration follows frustration. But miracle
of miracles, out of this forest of frustrations there
usually emerges a well-adjusted and well-rounded
youngster, who will later think of his childhood as
the best years of his life.

Frustration and aggression are very much a
part of growing up. What matters to us as parents
is the way these aggressions can be healthfully
channeled, what can be permitted and what not,
and at what point aggression turns into irrepressible hostility, when a psychiatrist must step in
to avert more serious difficulties.

Many children act very much like pressure cook-
ers. As long as the cooker lets off a little steam at
a time, nothing violent will happen. But if the lid
is clamped down solidly, watch out. Children who
give vent to their normal aggressive drives in

some harmless way rarely get into serious trouble. Visitors to our clinic are sometimes mystified by the faces chalked on our much-used punching bag. The explanation is simple: Many of our children drew pictures of their father or mother on the bag, and then give it a good workout. While most children assume these aggressive roles subconsciously, others are surprisingly frank and fully understand the dynamics of why they enjoy it. One thirteen-year-old girl, when told it was time to go home, said to me: "I've got to hit that punching bag just once more. Otherwise, I don't think I can stand Mother another week." In her case, it was much better for her to work out her problems on a leather bag than on a mother who reacts to aggression with irrationality and violence.

Parental understanding can make all the difference in the world. An acquaintance of mine has a ten-year-old boy, who recently managed to break three windowpanes in one swoop by slamming a kitchen door in a fit of fury. "You must really be very angry, Danny," said his mother in a reasonably calm voice, "but you just can't go around breaking windows. Let's talk about it." It proved a very wise response. Not only did mother and son get to the bottom of his frustration, but the boy volunteered to pay for the windows. It was the response and compassion of the mother to which the child responded.

Frustration must find some outlet of expression —but not at the cost of three windowpanes. If you help your child to feel that it is not wrong to feel anger, but you yourself know how to handle it when it comes, both you and he will be happier people.

Inevitably we come to the matter of Permissiveness. I always try to maintain a sense of humor about the whole concept. So much nonsense has been written and spoken about it. In the true sense of the word permissiveness really only means "the quality of permitting, of not forbidding or hindering." Anarchy in the home is not the result of parental permissiveness, but parental neglect. For the prudent parent, permissiveness sets certain bonds and certain limits, certain goalposts and endlines, within which the youngster is reasonably free to roam.

I would strongly advise parents against permissiveness, if the word means "the run of the house." The first milestone in achieving a true permissive parent-and-child relationship will be achieved once the essentials of obedience and discipline have been firmly established. An alarming number of homes today provide an environment which can be described as nothing less than chaotic. The results are only too apparent in the schools and the streets of our country.

Most parents search earnestly for a middle course. Much of their uncertainty in this important area stems from too little understanding of the relationship of obedience to discipline and to general educational principles. A great number of today's children who strike out with excessive aggressiveness do so without any guilt whatsoever. Children *should* feel guilty whenever they exceed the limits their parents an society have set up for them. Healthy guilt is a good and honest feeling, and a vital psychic governing device for the child's control over his own aggressions. Parents must create a conscience in their children to which they will hold.

I recognize that some parents find it difficult to relate willing child obedience to parental love. Nonetheless, the two are closely enmeshed. The child derives his ability to tell right from wrong from his parents. Once a child is six years old, he is usually able to make many of his own value judgments on the basis of what he *thinks* his parents would consider right or wrong. But in the absence of parental love, this natural process of evaluation is hardly possible. Without love, obedience to the child becomes a mere abstraction. Love must always precede obedience. The typical delinquent does not obey. For one important reason at least: he is not loved, nor has he ever known love.

In a sound educational environment, obedience and discipline are not regarded by the child as either odious or oppressive. On the contrary, he regards them as highway markers on a safe and happy road to maturity. The true function of education in the hands of the parent has rarely been better expressed than by Freud when he wrote:

"Let us get a clear idea of the primary business of what education is. The child has to learn to control his instincts. To grant it complete freedom, so that it obeys all its impulses without any restriction, is impossible for the parents and would do serious damage to the children themselves, as would be seen partly at the time and partly during subsequent years. The function of education therefore is to inhibit, forbid, suppress, and it has at all times carried out this function to admiration. But we have learned from analysis that it is this very suppression of instincts that involves the danger of neurotic illness. Education has therefore to steer its way between the Scylla of giving the instincts free play and the Charybdis of frustrating them. Unless the problem is altogether insoluble, an optimum of education must be discovered, which will do the most good and the least harm. It is a matter of finding out how much we may forbid, at which times and by what method."[2]

Finding out just how much we may forbid becomes possible only from a full understanding of our children. When the parent is in tune with the child's needs, when he or she is able to be sufficiently sensitive to the limits of his frustrations, matters of education as well as discipline fall into their proper place. It is only the rejected child who is unwilling or unable to accept frustration and discipline. This is the child who strikes out, who has little to gain from being obedient. He only wants to retaliate and punish his parents. But even for the normal child, this conflict between his aggressiveness and his adherence to parental rules crops up frequently. It is not always easily resolved. The normal child, however, will ultimately surrender his aggressions in return for something he considers more worthwhile. Normal children also learn, with their parents' understanding and cooperation, to work out aggressions in healthy and acceptable ways. Sports, hobbies, school debating, family activities and duties, all are healthy outlets which the wise parent will try to supply in ample measure.

Here are two practical investments which will immeasurably improve your chances of successfully dealing with childhood aggressions. A piece of linoleum, tacked to the wall of a child's room, will give him an opportunity to paint, carve, or stick pins into it without offense or damage to anyone or anything. Small boys, who are fond of hitting their fathers half in fun, but who perhaps are also acting out quite normal aggressions, will welcome a set of boxing gloves. Boxing gloves make fathers just a little less anxious about that sharp jab to the thigh, but they also label this childish sparring as play, allowed to last as long as the gloves are on.

Some parents feel that the only way they will ever keep their children's aggressions under control is to be within sight and sound of them at all times. This is of course hopelessly unrealistic. One mother of an overly aggressive eight-year-old boy recently said to me in utter desperation: "But I can't keep my eye on him *all* the time!" I had the feeling that the lid threatened to blow off any time, unless this mother was sitting on top of it. Parents who think they are controlling their overly aggressive children in this manner are in the long run only fooling themselves.

If governing devices on aggressive behavior are imposed in the early years of life, later childhood aggressions will have their own dampening mechanisms built in. We are speaking here of the child's conscience or superego. The superego, we might remember, represents a set of values. To the child it triggers an inner warning when a conflict begins to arise. When the deed has already occurred, guilt and remorse are a natural consequence, if the superego functions normally. In other words, when the "violation" has taken place, a warning flag goes up, which gives the youngster the uneasy feeling that he has not done the right thing, and that his parents will heartily disapprove. Sometimes, I can clarify the role of the superego in the child to parents by labeling it the "guardian angel in charge of good conduct," who incidentally has a full-time job watching over the youngster, who would just as soon have his guardian angel look the other way.

The well-developed superego will needle and nag him to the point where the misdeed is rarely worth the candle. Smaller children especially can often be overheard mumbling to themselves, muttering words like "naughty, naughty" or "don't touch." This is a dialogue between the two sides of the child's nature, between what the child would like to do and what he thinks he ought to do. The dialogue, even if silent, is pretty much contained through life. It keeps adults, as well as children, from doing the things which they know to be wrong, or, having done them, prevents their recurrence.

When this superego acts either too weakly or too tardily, we may have a delinquent child. Whether the misdeed is insignificant or truly destructive, most delinquents simply are unable to tell right from wrong. The distinctions blur, and deviate behavior becomes an almost foregone conclusion.

Much of the initial fault for the child's inability to build a firm superego must be the responsibility of the parent. I have seen too many parents fail dismally in building for their children in early life the kind of standards of right or wrong which are essential to laying the foundation of a conscience. Far too many parents abdicate their role to the neighborhood, to the school, and to other children, to provide this essential framework. They live in a fool's paradise. Time and time again, the weakness, or total absence of a delinquent's superego can be laid at the doorstep of the parents' disinterest in the child. The kind of life his parents live provides the strongest building blocks for the child's superego. Parents who are negligent will find that their children must of necessity make up their own codes of conduct, their own Do's and Don'ts. If these are at odds with what the outside world accepts as normal and moral, it is not the children's fault alone.

How do we distinguish between those aggressions which must be considered normal and those that are not? How do we recognize the child that strikes out, and at what point in the child's development must we become concerned? For parents who have overtly aggressive children, this can be a vital question.

One father of an overly aggressive boy remarked, "I guess the only way to stand Bobby is to understand him." Understand him he did, and Bobby's aggressions are now totally tolerable, compared to the year before. Bobby's father's reaction, however, is not typical. Too many parents still meet aggression with aggression. If by some miracle they could look ahead, they would see that this is folly. The festering emotional sores will never quite heal in either parent or child, and aggression will become a way of life for both.

Where aggression becomes part of a family pattern, a reasonable solution grows increasingly impossible. One of my patients, eleven-year-old Paul K., is so surrounded by hostility that his own aggressions are easily matched by his parents. In Paul's family, aggression feeds on aggression. His mother and father are truculent and hostile toward each other as well as toward their children. Against such a background, we can see why Paul considers aggression a normal pattern of life. His parents' behavior seems to sanction the validity of solving even the slightest frustration through counter-aggression.

Not only has all this added up to a chaotic way of life for Paul's entire family, but Paul himself is having a very difficult time adjusting to his school and his community, where his patterns of life are not accepted. Such home patterns are exceedingly difficult to break. Obviously, Paul's problems will never be solved until his parents find some solutions of their own. Their only present solution is to send Paul away to boarding school. No one knows better than Paul himself that he can now count himself one of our many unwanted children.

Within earshot of all of us live families where the back of the hand is the considered solution to bringing up "well-behaved" children. I myself know otherwise seemingly intelligent parents who will from time to time "beat some sense" into their youngsters because of some overstepping of the line. Others go even further and apply a thrashing as a "preventive" measure. What these parents fail to realize is that they introduce to their children the dreadful world in which Might is Right. When they are adults these children will take out their own aggressions not only on their fellowmen, but on their own children. Can we guess the response of this second generation?

Parental inhumanity toward children paints an appalling picture of its own. The worst kind of parental transgression is the surprisingly large number of parents who beat their small helpless babies. Several thousand babies each year die at the hand of their parents. But the true extent of this problem is difficult to ascertain. "If we had the real figures," says Dr. Frederic N. Silverman, a Cincinnati radiologist, who is studying the national problem of child abuse, "the total could easily surpass auto accidents as a killer and maimer of chidren." We know that one out of every ten babies beaten by its parents will die, and many more will suffer permanent brain damage.

Physical violence is not the cure for overaggressive children. I can fully sympathize with the parent's occasional temptation. Overtly aggressive children, quite frankly, can be singularly unattractive, and it takes all the patience and understanding of a parent to exert restraint.

How exactly, and from where, comes this impulse on the part of the child to be excessively aggressive? The true behavior problem child is narcissistic and demanding. His whole world revolves around him. He exists to satisfy his own whims and desires. He constantly makes demands and expect them to be met. When he feels aggressive he acts aggressively. He gives full rein to his impulses, which are never diminished by the guilt feelings of better adjusted youngsters. While the withdrawn child expresses his problems through anxiety, this child expresses his through aggression. Such children will regard any punishment meted out to them as unfair and a further expression of the small regard the world has for them. Such punishments are never forgotten. They will vow to "get even" some other time.

Unhappily, they often respond poorly to psychiatric treatment. Much of the relevancy of life is gone for them. The aggressive child discriminates little between one person and the next. He is afraid and distrustful of everyone. This wall of hostility is difficult to crack. To do so takes high professional skill and the patience of both therapist and parent.

Aggression in children manifests itself in many ways. Some, while acceptable at an earlier age, become serious indicators of trouble when continued into the later years. Temper tantrums, for example, are perfectly normal at two, but can be a serious danger sign at ten or twelve.

The distinctions are important. To the very young child, temper tantrums provide the means to express his anger. They frequently represent a loss of self-control so typical at that age. We cannot expect more of the two-year-old, nor should we make any serious attempts to block his tantrums. If we do, frustration patterns can set themselves up throughout the later years as well.

We do, however, expect much better performance in the case of the older child. Whenever I encounter a preadolescent or adolescent who bursts into irrepressible temper tantrums, it is almost always a sign of truly aggressive feelings about a world which he may hate and certainly does not love.

Such youngsters are not at all uncommon these days. Uncontrolled temper tantrums occur in children of all ages, but often are most pronounced and serious in adolescence. Mary Lou was such a child. A fourteen-year-old girl, Mary Lou was brought to our clinic by her parents, because she "constantly flies off the handle." For no apparent reason, according to her parents, Mary Lou lapsed into violent tantrums in almost daily succession. She did not get along with her father nor with her two younger sisters. Mary Lou did poorly in school. She had often expressed the wish to die. Her parents were shocked and saddened by their own sense of failure.

Mary Lou's case turned out to be extremely complex. We knew from a long series of interviews with all family members that we were faced with a difficult home environment. Mary Lou as the firstborn had been a badly spoiled baby. But when her two sisters arrived, the parents' major attention was focused increasingly on them. Mary Lou felt left out of things. She became increasingly disobedient and grossly disrespectful, particularly toward her father.

The parents' reaction was interesting. Mary Lou's hot temper, according to her father, was largely inherited from her mother. "She also flies off the handle," he told us. We found the mother to be exceedingly obsessed with discipline and with strict child-rearing. Until Mary Lou was thirteen, no socializing outside of school was permitted. The father, who had always wanted a boy, placed demands on Mary Lou which a girl found difficult to accept. He would ask her to cut the lawn, to paint the house, even to mix concrete.

In addition to these demands and restrictions, Mary Lou's home life was extremely confining. Her mother insisted, for example, that Mary Lou keep the door of her room wide open at all times. (Most little girls like to create their own privacy for at least some of the time.) When Mary Lou persisted in closing her door, her mother had it unhinged. There were other examples of unreasonable discipline. After Mary Lou had repeatedly forgotten to switch off the light when she left her room, her mother removed the bulb. As a matter of family policy, her parents refused to drive her to any school functions. She had to rely on neighbors and classmates. What her parents did not know was that Mary Lou has been secretly dating a juvenile delinquent. What had begun as an expression of resentment against parents restrictions had resulted in a strong attachment to the boy. Today "blowing off steam" is Mary Lou's way of expressing her frustrations. It does not require much insight to foresee the course of events. If we had reached Mary Lou when she was six, rather than fourteen, we could have done more for her and her parents.

Temper tantrums are one of the more dramatic outlets for hostility and anger. They also attract attention, but rarely have the auspicious results the child expects. A most common form of aggressive pattern, less dramatic than tantrums, can be seen at school. When the disciplinary clamps are on tight in the home, the school often receives the butt of the child's aggressions.

Not long ago, a father and mother consulted me about their six-year-old boy. It was obvious that they came with the utmost reluctance. Billy had just been expelled from school. Expulsion from the first grade is unusual. It connotes an impossible situation, a last resort for the school authorities. Billy was a very bright boy, but he proved totally unmanageable. His parents, however, could not understand the school's justification for expulsion. "Billy had always been a perfect boy," his father told us. "He had to be: we'd never permit him to be anything else."

On the surface, at least, the school seemed to have made a harsh decision. But Billy's parents turned out to have rigid and authoritative personalities. Neither was particularly blessed with human warmth and compassion. For six years, Billy had lived "according to the book." This had meant strict schedules for sleeping, playing, and eating. When Billy cried, his parents "let him cry it out," and the comforting hand of his mother or father rarely touched his shoulder or his cheek. The parents told us that thumb-sucking, toilet-training, and bed-wetting had been solved successfully, mostly through threats of punishment, when lapses did occur. Nonetheless, they admitted, both sucking and soiling returned at frequent intervals, for which he received punishment, often physical. It was only in school, away from his parents, that Billy dared let go of his pent-up aggressions. The school administration and teachers, trained in such matters, recognized Billy for what he was. Not a bad child, but a sick one. In the case of Billy, the prognosis now looks good. He ought to be back in school in a short time.

Eleven-year-old Virginia had similar problems —but hers had a reverse twist: This girl was a model student in class, but turned into what her mother referred to as "a holy terror" at home. Virginia was constantly making unreasonable demands. She was self-absorbed and given to violent temper tantrums whenever her wishes were not immediately acceded to.

Part of the difficulty seemed to rest with the parents as individuals. Virgina's mother seemed a rather detached woman. Subsequently we learned that she had had serious emotional problems with her own mother and older sister from an early age, which remained unresolved. Her sister had been favored by her father throughout her childhood. This not only had remained in her memory, but had colored all of her subsequent relations with women, including her own daughter, Virginia.

Virginia's father, on the other hand, seemed to play a minor role: He was away on business much of the time, and Virginia saw little of him. Nonetheless, according to the mother, her husband had always preferred Virginia to herself. Virginia's mother, whose basic problem seemed an inability to relate genuinely to another woman, was assigned to a female therapist, with whose help she gained considerable insight into her own problems and their specific impact on her daughter. Virginia herself was assigned to another therapist—a warm, affectionate mother figure—who now acts as a temporary mother substitute until Virginia's mother can provide the kind of close relationship which both deserve. Both mother and daughter have been seen twice weekly for almost a year.

We are about to cut down to a once-a-week schedule. Both are making excellent progress in achieving a much closer relationship to one another.

Parents are often concerned about their children's lying and stealing. Both habits are not uncommon and often offer no grounds for serious concern. Both the child's age as well as circumstances play a role here. When a child is small, lying is usually a matter of stating things inaccurately, touched often by the need for fantasy. When your five-year-old tells you that he has fifty dollars in his pocket, he has probably overheard you saying it to someone else. You should not be worried. Obviously, your youngster has not the faintest idea of what fifty dollars looks like.

We should also remember that some children live in more of a fairy-tale world than others. Parents should never ridicule or laugh at its inhabitant. Sooner or later, however, they should make it clear to their children that important differences exist between the make-believe and the real world.

When these habits persist in the later years, however, the situation is no longer normal. Nor is the child. The persistent stealer and liar is a child with serious problems. The discovery of such serious deviate behavior often leaves parents in a state of shock. Other parents react by laughing off such exploits as "kid stuff." When such things happen repeatedly at age ten, twelve, or fourteen, it is no longer kid stuff at all. I recall a mother, a woman of means, who came to tell me rather sheepishly that her maid had just discovered a closet-full of "loot," accumulated by her nine-year-old daughter, Pamela. Pamela had denied all, but could offer no satisfactory explanation as to how penknives, transister radios, and costume jewelry happened to get there. Her parents could easily afford to provide their daughter with all of these trinkets.

We soon came to what we felt to be the root of the problem: Both parents were professional people, absent from home much of the time. Pamela had assumed for years that behind her parents' usual absence lay their rejection of her. Her parents had never taken any pains to explain to her the real reasons for their being away much of the time, let alone question whether these long absences were good for the child.

Pamela's parents also happened to be strict disciplinarians. They enforced a rigorous routine in the brief periods they were at home. As a way of getting even with a world which (Pamela thought) hardly recognized her existence, the child began to take small items from her luckier classmates, who were getting more out of life than she. Typical of the aggressive child who strikes out, Pamela exhibited no guilt feelings. Her parents, on the other hand, took the discovery badly, especially after the cause and effect relationship between their own negligence and Pamela's thefts became clear to them.

Is habitual child theft invariably a difficult problem to cure? Not necessarily, if the parents have sufficient insight into the over-all dynamics. Many cases of child theft can be handled right in the home, without the need of therapy. For those parents who feel that they can solve their youngster's problems, a few rules of thumb should be observed. First of all, parents should make it a point never to let stealing work out to the child's advantage. No reward for the return of an item must be offered or given, and, in the event the stolen object is lost, the child should replace it out of earned effort, if he is old enough.

When children are caught in the act, or faced with the goods, the situation should always be frankly handled. The child will usually get over the shock of the confrontation, and may indeed secretly feel relieved at having been discovered. If parents seem unable to arrive at a genuine solution to their child's theft problems, however, they will be far wiser to seek professional help.

A far deeper and more serious problem is the child that kills or threatens to kill. The thought seems inconceivable and absurd. And yet, at least a brief reference to child murder belongs in any discussion of the child who strikes out, since it occurs more frequently than most of us care to realize. The basic problem is usually the parent and not the child. In a study of hundreds of child-killer cases, Lucy Freeman and Dr. Wilfred C. Hulse summarize, "What they all had in common was a psychologically poverty-stricken back-ground. When it is a matter of murder, not money but devotion counts. These children lacked paren-tal love, guidance and respect."[3]

For every murder a child commits, ten children consider the act seriously. Many children come closer to murder than the world knows. While writing these pages, I received a call from a priest, asking me to see a fourteen-year-old boy imme-diately. The priest, who fortunately had some psychiatric training in his background, had heard Larry express his intention of killing his father the following weekend. The priest, rightly sensed that the boy was too emotionally ill to shrink from such a deed. Fortunately, the deed did not follow the wish.

Although a potential murderer, Larry is char-acteristic of many youngsters who are given little chance to develop into normal human beings.

Throughout his fourteen years, Larry had been brutally manhandled by his father. His mother was in constant terror of her husband's violence, and insisted that both she and Larry appease him under all circumstances. Subsequent interviews showed that the father was curiously unaware of his wife's and son's true feelings toward him. As happens so often, the father himself was seriously emotionally disturbed. Fourteen years of terror are difficult to wipe away from a boy's memory. Larry now is so seriously ill that he is in a state hospital. We cannot yet tell what may become of him.

In less severe cases of overt aggression for the child who steals, throws temper tantrums, the child who lies, the child who screams, and the child who sets fires and destroys property, the help which they can receive today promises better results. The aggressive child, we must remember, is at war with himself as well as the world. The earlier parents recognize the symptoms and accept the fact that their child may need help the earlier the child may resume a normal and healthy life.

Also to be remembered is the fact that much of juvenile delinquency of the adolescent, discussed elsewhere, has its true beginnings in the first ten years of life. An eight-year-old boy, with built-in aggressions and hostility, has to take only one short step into the adolescent gang delinquency a few years hence. Unless we have helped him solve some of his basic problems of hostility by the time he reaches the precarious point of adolescent turbulence, we will not have done all that could have been done for him.

The child who destroys for the fun of destroying usually does so because of some inner emotional conflict. Children who perform such "harmless" acts as putting tacks under car tires, flooding the bathroom, or setting fire to the garage need their parents' help. Defiance and hostility of deep significance usually underlie such behavior.

In summary, the problem of the aggressive child is often the problem of the aggressive parent. Help is often needed by both. If I return time and again to the subject of early detection and early treatment, it is only because time is on the side of the child. But he must be given the time early enough.

The rules are simple and dramatically vivid: Aggression begets aggression, hostility begets hostility, and love begets love. Who will make the first move, the parent or the child? Time, parents will discover, runs out very quickly.

Let not pride interfere with making the first move. This, too, is part of maturity. If there is ever to be a world without hate, it will be because, at one very crucial moment, enough parents will have decided that understanding and loving the ones closest to them are more important than anything else in life, pride being the least significant.

Your child understands little about pride. But he cares a great deal about your love.

It is really as simple as all that.

1 Social history and background.
2 Freud, Sigmund, *New Introductory Lectures in Psychoanalysis*, pp. 203-204, Norton, New York, 1933.
3 Lucy Freeman and Wilfred C. Hulse, *Children Who Kill*, Berkley Medallion Books, New York, 1962, p. 158.

XI

Trouble in School

OF ALL CHILDHOOD emotional disturbances, none occur more frequently than emotional blocks to learning. We broadly define these as "learning disabilities." Educators refer to such children as "underachievers."

A learning disability, to put it simply, describes a child's inability to perform satisfactorily the schoolwork for which he is intellectually equipped. By clinical definition, a child who falls two or more grades behind his normal grade level in one or more learning skills—be it reading, spelling, or arithmetic—suffers an acute and definite learning disability.

For an emotionally disturbed youngster the onset of a learning disability may represent an emotional Waterloo. For a time, even seriously disturbed children may manage to get by from one year to the next. Acute crisis points may be skirted or entirely avoided. But once the more structured obligations of formal school life begin in earnest, even otherwise controlled emotional problems quickly rise to the surface. As a consequence, some drastic action by the school and the parent often becomes urgent and unavoidable.

Why should school seem to trigger such serious problems? For the first time in the child's life, the teacher imposes certain external patterns of expectation, discipline, and work habits. Major adjustments to school life are made by normal children. As the months and years go by, however, children with emotional blocks to learning become increasingly easy to identify. When even the minimum school criteria fail to be met, some deep-seated emotional problem often lingers under the surface, requiring treatment before the blocks, hopefuly, may be removed.

I am under the distinct impression that today childhood learning disabilities have reached epidemic proportions. Several million youngsters now show clear-cut cases of emotional learning blocks. Other millions suffer similar handicaps, although in their case the basic cause is not emotional, but physical or socio-cultural in nature.

Learning problems form the major element of the nation's appalling rate of high school dropouts. An estimated 7.5 million youngsters are expected to drop out of school in the next ten years. These failures represent a terrible waste of human manpower, and a failure by society, as well as the individual. Too many of these children sooner or later become involved in some criminal act. For example, one-half of the arrests for burglaries and larcenies and almost two-thirds of all auto thefts now involve persons under eighteen years of age. Eighty-five percent of all adults in prison, according to the FBI, entered a life of crime before they were nineteen.

One of our great hopes is to return dropouts to school, and by detecting the still greater number of potential dropouts, to provide them with whatever help may be indicated. I know a number of young-potential dropouts, to provide them with whatever help may be indicated. I know a number of youngsters through direct experience whom psychiatric help has kept in school. All over the nation, well-planned guidance programs are reaching an increasing number of young people.

Unfortunately, learning disabilities are complex and often difficult to treat. Parents need to know just what these involve, and how they may be treated. Basically, your child's learning disabilities can be viewed in three broad causative categories:

1. While your child may have the intellectual capacity, he may be unable to use it effectively because of some deep-seated emotional problem. I include here also cultural and environmental problems, such as negative self-concepts and poor attitudes toward education generally.

2. The basic cause of your child's learning disability may be physical, rather than emotional, in nature. He may suffer from some neurological or undetected physical handicap. He may suffer from impaired vision or hearing, some maturational lag, or he may be paying the consequences of a prolonged school absence caused by illness. A deep-seated state of lassitude due to some physical cause, or some brain damage, may also be the cause of a learning disability.

3. Lastly, learning disabilities can be caused by certain contemporary sociological syndromes. These are increasingly common and are of vital concern. That overcrowded classrooms or incompetent teachers sometimes exist should not be overlooked. Children may also fall victims to excessive parental as well as social pressures to compete for excellence throughout their entire school span. Here, it is not psychiatric care that will turn the tide, but a more sobering view of what education is all about. It may require changed parental attitudes, or perhaps some corrective action within the school environment itself.

Learning disabilities never "break out" all of a

sudden. Unlike German measles, the road of the underachiever covers a long period of time. While its causes may be multiple, the pattern itself follows familiar lines: Your child begins school. You send him off with high hopes. He is bright, and he seems "ready" for school. The first few months pass uneventfully enough. To be sure, he says little about school. This is common.

Then his teacher begins to report that he is not functioning as she thinks he should. The word "underachieving" begins to creep into conversations. He is underachieving, the teacher says, which you suppose really still leaves things on the hopeful side. He is, after all, obviously capable of doing more. Unhappily, as the semesters go by, the achievement gap widens. Reading and arithmetic seem to lag particularly, no matter how much time you and the teacher devote to him. Repeating the second grade doesn't help, either. Finally, the school advises help.

Very often this is the way it happens. The reason you have not acted before this is also understandable: You have pitted hope against hope that time will be all he needs.

It is hardly consoling to know that if your child has a learning problem, he is not alone: an estimated 10 percent of all children require special assistance for various forms of classes in different parts of the country brought out the fact that 22.6 percent of all children studied suffered some reading disability. In another study of twelve thousand students in ninety New York State school districts, the bright students who dropped out of high school before graduation did so primarily because of emotional problems.

One of the more curious aspects of school underachievers is the fact that the overwhelming percentage are boys. Learning disabilities occur eight to ten times more frequently with boys than with girls. We can only speculate why this is so. It is still generally true that fewer demands are placed on girls in terms of their need to succeed in school as a stepladder to college, a career, and a vocation. The boys perhaps bear another burden: It is usually more difficult for mothers to accept their boys' natural aggressions. We know that many boys consequently try to repress their aggressions and often rebel, unconsciously, through learning disabilities.

Differences in the rapidity with which boys and girls mature physically, neurologically, as well as emotionally, also give girls a considerable natural edge. Girls, as girls, often seem far better prepared for learning at any given time than their brothers.

Many parents postpone seeking help for their child's learning disability until the cards are staked high against the child. Unfortunately, psychiatry has not advanced to the point where we can point with any pride to the wide and general effectiveness of treatment of emotionally caused learning disorders. My own experience as well as that of other therapists indicates that our success is very meager indeed. One reason why we often tend to make so little headway is the fact that by the time many children reach us, the underlying emotional problem is deep-rooted and of long duration.

In this day and age, when educational excellence and solid school achievements have become both family and national goals, parents live under particular pressures to see their child compete and succeed. Learning problems, therefore, are nowadays particularly difficult to accept. Even parents who do accept them sometimes remain reluctant to seek psychiatric advice for fear of discovering things about themselves, which they would just as soon leave untouched and unrealized.

I sympathize with this reluctance, but always remind parents how terribly important it is for them to face up early to all potential problem areas for the sake of their child.

I can do no more than urge parents to try to get to the nub of the problem just as soon as they begin to suspect difficulties.

Whether the cause is institutional, physical, or emotional, it can usually be determined by the relatively simple process of elimination. Your child's teacher, school counselor, and pediatrician can be immensely valuable here.

Is the cause physical? Psychiatric treatment will not return your child to 20-20 vision, but a pair of corrective glasses can. Conversely, sound therapy may very well extend the attention span of a child who does have perfect vision, but who cannot concentrate on the blackboard for some deep-seated emotional reason .

Is the teacher the culprit? Is it no longer very likely. A really poor teacher is rapidly becoming a rarity, although a child who cannot relate to the teacher is not. Whenever I hear parents blaming their child's school problems on his teacher, I immediately ask how many "poor teachers' Johnny has had in the last four years. When I hear them say that none had been good, I suspect the common problem-denominator to be Johnny, and not the four "bad" teachers.

Constitutional as well as physiological handicaps often cause secondary emotional repercussions. For example, a child who suffers from any undetected blood or vitamin deficiency may very well create for himself emotional reactions, as he begins to fall behind his schoolmates.

I have also seen parents mistake physical causes for emotional ones. Let me illustrate. Twelve-year-old Nora was one of my most short-term patients. Nora was doing increasingly poorly in school. She had tested out as a bright child, but something held her back from doing the kind of work her school expected of her. Repeated talks revealed no distinct emotional disturbance, except a pronounced shyness and distinct lack of self-confidence. One day while Nora was waiting at the clinic to have her mother pick her up, I happened to see her squinting her eyes to gaze out of the window. As it turned out, Nora had suffered from poor eyesight for several years. But eyeglasses, Nora was convinced, would make her unattractive. She was grimly determined to keep the fact from her family. A year had gone by—with ever-diminishing school marks—trying to read blackboard assignments which she could hardly decipher, let alone understand.

I remember Billy as quite a similar and equally common case. Billy was a charming fifteen-year-old boy. He had suffered from an acute hearing disability for three years before anyone ever became aware of his trouble. It was only his increasingly dismal school performance which finally caused his parents to stir. A thorough medical checkup disclosed a definite hearing problem which had existed for some time. The prospect of having his schoolmates ridicule his hearing aid was enough for him to want to keep his hearing problems to himself.

The essential framework of the learning process involves two basic principles: The first is Capacity, the second Motivation. Capacity relates directly to the intellectual, neurological, and physical ability to perform within a normal school environment. Nora's and Billy's capacities were impaired because of serious physical deficiencies.

Motivation, on the other hand, is concerned with emotion. Both good motivation and good capacity must be present if learning is to be successfully absorbed. A youngster may be motivated to pay attention in class and perform his schoolwork, because to do so offers the pleasurable rewards of parental and teacher approval. Not to do so may invite humiliation, embarrassment, perhaps even withdrawal of affection.

Unfortunately, everything else one may wish to say about emotional blocks to learning grows less and less simple. "Why can't my child read?" parents want to know. The answers, unfortunately, will vary as many times as there are children. Each child with a learning disability presents us with a new set of personal history, environment, and psychological makeup. When combined, they create emotional learning blocks of almost unique characteristics.

Most non-learners, we find, exhibit extremes of repressed aggression or submission. This basic observation, that behind almost every reading and learning problem there lurks some deeply felt aggression or frustration, can best be illustrated by two simple cases: A young boy with an I.Q. of 126 has failed his third grade twice, and now reads no better than he did two years ago. The cause? Throughout his young life, his father had been an inveterate reader, habitually preferring his books to the boy. To the boy, books were his greatest enemy, and he reacted by unconsciously refusing to learn to read.

Another case clearly illustrates the element of

extreme submission: A nine-year-old boy was bright and otherwise seemed to perform quite well. He also had a fair brighter older brother, who consistently garnered straight A's in arithmetic, receiving all kinds of attention for his superior performance. Perhaps only total school failure, the nine-year-old thought, could draw parental attention to him for a while.

Children who fail in their studies regard the learning challenge with varying degrees of anxiety. It is indeed difficult sometimes to separate cause from effect: Severe emotional upsets, even in adults, will create learning blocks and weaken the power of concentration. Conversely, the inability to perform—whatever its causes—can create anxieties which can become serious psychological burdens.

While inner anxieties represent a frequent cause of learning disorders, we must also look closely at the kind of relationship a child has with his parents. This directly relates to the motivation and self-confidence with which a child enters his formal learning environment. This cause-and-effect mechanism is particularly true in the case of the mother. She is a child's first teacher. Far more than the father, she represents the prime directing force for the child. After the first year (when the maternal function is to cater and to care, rather than to instruct and direct) the manner in which the mother relates to her child in the learning process can condition the child positively or negatively toward the more structured learning environment of grammar school.

When we look at the mother-child relationship with regard to learning, several principles emerge. The first revolves around the kind of person the mother is. If she is a highly authoritarian person, the child may rebel at least silently, perhaps to pass through years of passive resistance. In the transition from a powerful mother-teacher to the school-teacher period, all persons who tell such a child what to do and what to think may become authority figures. Very often, the child will resist in overt ways, one of the best of which is not to pay attention.

In contrast, I know some mothers whose extreme passivity and anxiety produce in their children learning problems which mirror the particular emotional life of the mother. Such women go through life denying anger, making a great effort to appear sweet to the point of being saccharine, denying every negative and aggressive drive, and on the surface at least appearing to live a life of perfect serenity and perfection. The child with such a mother as his life-model will often encounter serious problems when he faces a school curriculum which inevitably contains a certain amount of frustration and anxiety. Such children, in their effort not to lose the love of their mother, will often reflect their mother's attitude and avoid responsibilities and deny that any school challenges exist. Faced with a choice, these children quite naturally prefer to be loved, rather than to achieve. Hence the child may very well treat studying as his mother treats life: uninvolved, non-emotional and non-engaging, showing a total lack of participation.

One of my little boy patients fits this description perfectly: When Paul first came to see me, I was struck by his charm and almost excessive gaiety. Unlike most youngsters, he avoided the punching ball in our playroom, stayed away from all guns, soldiers, and Indians. He preferred to sit quietly in a corner and read a book. Paul consistently assured me that everything was going "fine" in school. I knew from the school authorities that he was performing far below his true capacities.

Paul's mother exhibited an almost identical behavior pattern. She appeared to be extremely pleasant and friendly without the slightest tinge of aggression or antagonism. Even when I purposefully tried to prod her with a challenging remark to attempt some measurement of her frustration level, she entirely overlooked my point. A normal reaction would have been to reply sharply.

The point of our therapy is to have Paul's mother see that anxieties can be acknowledged and tolerated, and that expressions of aggression are at times healthy and quite acceptable. Once the mother begins to retort to my proddings, and Paul no longer avoids the punching bag, we will have made progress in helping him cope with his learning difficulties.

A second vital principle concerns the attitudes of the mother toward her school child. So very frequently, we come across mothers who find it exceedingly difficult to "let go" of their school-age children. Many such mothers are themselves unhappy individuals. Frequently they are failures as marriage partners, or frustrated in some of their life's ambitions. All the essence of their love and devotion then boils down and focuses on their child. We often see the rather abnormal obsession of a parent to prolong, at all costs, an extremely close but unwholesome parent-child relationship. When a mother's whole life is centered upon her six-year-old son, his departure for school may represent an almost cataclysmic emotional experience.

Even in less extreme cases, mothers unconsciously feel the school as a keen competitor. We must remember that though all of this may be carried on unconsciously, the emotions form powerful motivating drives. They should not be underestimated, even though they may be consciously denied. If it does grow into a conflict between the child's allegiance to his mother and his allegiance to his school, it becomes quite tempting for a mother not to encourage school success. Such drives are often strongly supported by the child himself, especially if he shares a strong and close relationship with his mother. Too successful a school performance, after all, may connote too firm a school allegiance.

Many mothers unconsciously try to control this school allegiance to the detriment of the youngster's learning abilities. Let us take a typical day in the life of Mary Strong, stouthearted mother of six-year-old Richie. Everything that Richie is today, Mary has convinced herself, is due to her. The boy couldn't do or be anything without her benign and constant influence. Now, Richie returns from school. He absentmindedly kisses his mother's cheek, excitedly opens his schoolbag to show her how well he is doing in his class assignments. But contrary to expectation, Mary's forced smile hides her inner chagrin. She isn't really happy. Richie, she knows, did this all on his own. For the first time in her life, he did not need her.

I illustrate the point because, to the neurotic person, even a ludicrous life situation can appear tragic. Like many other people with weak egos and strong neuroses, Mary Strong now faces a triangle: herself, her son Richie, and his school. It is Richie's school, not *her* school. The balance is no longer one to one. It is now two to one.

What about youngsters such as Richie? One can easily imagine what can happen. For the child dependent upon his mother's love and attention, maintaining a close relationship can take high priority over the demands of school. The reverse may also happen. For those children deprived of maternal attention, the opposite road may beckon: If he does poorly in school and is troubled by his homework, the mother is far more likely to devote time to him and offer almost unlimited attention.

The child learns soon enough that much depends on his ability to read. His mother agrees. Furthermore, *he* knows that his mother cares. Soon, the psychological equation reads as follows: "Difficulty in reading=mother's help and attention." This could evolve into the dangerous one of "reading failure=a surer love relationship with mother."

Learning difficulties have begun on less. Some parents, I know, scoff at the logic of such a train of thoughts. I can assure them that this is precisely the sequence of events from which some learning disabilities emerge. I have treated a number of young people, in whom, once having removed such a love-anxiety, the learning disability has disappeared.

An example of a more complex personal interrelationship which impinges on a learning disability can be seen through one of my patients, nine-year-old Art. Art's records show him to have an I.Q. of 119, classifying him as a bright boy. Nonetheless, Art shows serious learning disabilities and a school phobia. Art is retarded two years in both his reading and arithmetic. He often plays hookey from school. Even when in class he functions very poorly. Significantly, two years ago, Art's brother, Kevin, who is now eleven, was referred to me for strikingly similar difficulties.

An intimation of how complex the origin of a learning difficulty is seen by this family history.

Their parents' marriage had been a failure from the very beginning. Art's father is a passive and dependent man, given to alcohol and violent tempers. His relationship to his children is practically non-existent. The mother, finding no satisfaction in her conjugal relationship, devotes her entire life to her boys. Her total emotional satisfactions rest on them. The effect, from the boy's standpoint, is too much mother and too little father .

It takes little imagination to know what goes on in such a house. The parents quarrel frequently. Art's mother has often threatened to leave. Furthermore, everyone knew that she genuinely meant it, having on several occasions come to the point of packing a suitcase. Prolonged therapy with Art revealed that his daily return from school was almost always accompanied by a dread whether his mother would still be there when he opened the door. One can easily see how Art's absence from home, required by his school, could grow into a painful experience. These could easily evolve into emotional blocks to learning.

In Art's case as with so many others, little can be done about the learning disability without first improving the total family picture. Both parents as well as the two boys are now in therapy. Some progress is being made. If the mother and father come to a better understanding with each other, we can help Art begin to make some headway.

While I have primarily spoken of the mother's relationship to the school child, it is also true that the father can and should play a vital role in providing learning motivations for the child. The failure of Art's father as a husband and father only confirms the role of the father in regard to this particular disability.

In the broader sense, a learning disability represents essentially an ego-disability. In other words, a failure of the child to learn is a failure to regard himself with any substantive self-esteem. The view which a child has of himself is at least as strongly mirrored by the father as the mother. The father represents the main protection against the uncertainties of the outside world. It is the father who in most families faces the daily challenges, the frustrations and discouragements. It is also the father who, at least by implication of his life's work, says to his children, "It's a tough place, but as you can see, I can handle it, and so will you."

"I could not point to any need in childhood," said Freud, "as strong as that for a father's protection." For the six-year-old child, ready for that vast new experience called "school," both the protection of and identification with his father may become terribly vital and important. This holds equally for boys and girls. For the boy, his own masculine identification with his father represents one of the most natural and desirable self-supports imaginable. For the six-year-old girl, her special Oedipal relationship with her father virtually carries built-in admiration and stimulation.

Some parents mistakenly assume that a father's contribution to overcoming a child's learning failure is limited to helping him with his schoolwork. This in itself may or may not be useful, but it fails to get to the crux of the matter. Our pattern of living increasingly prevents the father from spending much time with his children. This need not necessarily prove significant so far as the child's development is concerned. What plays a far more vital role is the father's whole attitude toward himself, his family, and his purpose in life.

The father who has successfully answered the question of "Who Am I?" will quite readily find his sons and daughters endowed with a like sense of purpose. The challenges of school are then quite readily faced.

The father who had a bad day at the office and yet cheerfully returns the following day will find his child free and able to face the school's challenges and difficulties without regarding himself as a failure. Like his father, he will return the next day and face up to his school responsibilities. They may seem momentarily baffling, but nonetheless appear in manageable dimensions.

When fathers, however, lack such self-esteem and confidence as effective and successful human beings, their own children may grow more susceptible to developing learning disabilities. In a recent study of eighteen boys with learning disabilities, almost all of the boys' fathers turned out to be devoid of personal ambitions and regarded their current lives as failures, undervaluing their contributions to their families and society. Over half of them were college graduates. The readiness of these men to accept a self-derogatory role with helpless resignation was impressive.[1]

To the child of a passive father, his own learning disabilities may appear to be part of his normal environment. Men who go through life with an attitude of self-devaluation often carry on a dependent and totally passive relationship with their wives. Many such fathers can neither take pleasure in a boy's school accomplishments nor help him over a long period of time. They feel compelled to compete with their offspring for the attention of the mother. Under such family circumstances, the inadequacy of the father is often taken to be a fact of life by the whole family, including the father himself.

The child is then often constrained to remain a failure in order to hold his father's love. This is particularly true during his strong Oedipal period, when he will most strongly identify with his father. It is also quite evident to him that his mother prefers the passivity of the father. Such youngsters are thus encouraged to pattern their own behavior on that of their fathers.

Learning disabilities do not crop up only in children of passive fathers, of course. Aggressive fathers also leave their impact on the learning motivations of their children. The strong father, who makes good in business but has an ill-concealed "killer instinct" and exercises authority with barely controlled hostile aggression, often creates emotional problems in his children, for which he is least prepared.

The psychological dynamics here are interesting. The act of learning represents basically an act of acquisition. ("Hitting the books," "devouring knowledge," and "cramming" all connote acts of acquisition or aggression.) Youngsters with excessively aggressive fathers may easily confuse healthy aggressions (such as learning) with unhealthy and hostile aggressions which they may see in their father. "To achieve is to hurt" can become for them an at least unconscious equation.

There are many sons of particularly aggressive fathers who assume a totally passive and non-achieving role as a means of retaliating where they know they can hurt their fathers—the failure to achieve. In my view, it is not at all an accident that we find so many successful, competitive, and hard-driving men with dilatory, passive, and often introverted offspring. I happen to practice in a community with a particularly high percentage of successful men and "captains of industry," and have perhaps encountered more than a normal number of passive children.

Learning disabilities under such circumstances can be particularly severe. A good case in point is sixteen-year-old David. David's school performance is especially interesting: After one year in public school, David's parents transferred him from one private school to another. According to our records, he entered the first at age seven, the second at age eleven, and the third at age fifteen. Private tutors have been part of David's life for the past nine years. Despite all of the advantages of special schools and tutors, David at sixteen barely manages the schoolwork of a thirteen-year-old.

Other patterns of his behavior are also symptomatic of his particular learning disability. His social activities are far more restricted than those of other boys and girls of his age. He dates rarely. Seldom does he speak of his friends. We suspect that whatever friendships he has been able to develop are of short duration. His interests in sports, hobbies, and so forth, come and go at frequent intervals. They are never sustained. He is restive, showing no purpose or thought about his future career, college, or adult development.

The role of the father in this case is a crucial one. He is an extremely successful businessman. A highly competitive and aggressive personality combined with unusual intelligence, David's father has reached a top position in his company.

For a number of years, he has treated David like one of his employees. He has always assumed that David would follow in his footsteps in his profession. But the boy was repelled by the father's pattern of success "at-all-costs." The more the father pressed for perfection, the more David failed. The more tutors entered his life, the more he resisted all learning. The father, increasingly desperate, tried to "beat" learning into him. His usually controlled temper flared up frequently. He called his son "stupid" and a "lazy good-for-nothing." David soon came to believe that he was indeed stupid and destined to go nowhere. He assumed that since his father considered him stupid, so must the rest of the world.

Unconsciously, of course, David's underachieving became a silent weapon. The more he failed, the more he hurt his father. The more his father vituperated, the more he withdrew into his own inner life. "David sees the father," my psychiatric report says, "as a manipulator of people, an exhibitionist, one who handles himself well in social affairs." He woud like to express openly his resentment toward him, but he dare not. Instead, there is passive resistance, procrastination, apathy, mumbled speech, nail-biting, and a turning inward.

Illness, be it mental or physical, must be viewed in terms of its cause as well as its effect and possible complications. With learning disabilities, the later emotional complications can be severe. I think that most parents can perhaps more easily understand the practical implications of such learning difficulties, rather than the basic causes themselves.

What are some of the more important consequences of a learning disability? First of all, there is the obvious one of a poorly educated child. A child who for years has suffered from a reading disability may also suffer some permanent personality maladjustment. From the first school year onward, and for the rest of his life, the child exists in a competitive relationship to the rest of the world. A mounting failure to remain on an equal footing with his fellows can leave permanent psychic strains of inadequacy and insecurity.

Many children with learning disabilities may quite readily project this one important handicap onto their total view of themselves. This "self-concept," as we call it, may in the end prove so distorted and distant from the truth that it may create traumas of lifetime duration. A self-image of stupidity, rather than a specific inability to read or write well, can create individuals who function poorly as social beings. In our particular world they also find it increasingly difficult to eke out any kind of subsistence and are more prone to stray across the line of legality to commit a wide variety of felonious, even criminal acts.

The child with a prolonged and severe learning disability faces other problems: He may decide upon some anti-social behavior, or he may withdraw from the real world of challenge and competition. He can never hope to get into college, let alone matriculate successfully. The kind of employment open to him is increasingly restricted, and the view of himself as a worthwhile human may be permanently distorted. These can be some of the costs of a learning disability. The best solution, naturally, lies in prevention. This of course is of little solace to parents whose children have already developed a learning problem. As this discussion of learning disabilities has amply shown, the solutions to such problems are not always readily at hand. Often, they lie in quite different directions from those that seem most logical. I am firmly convinced that parents waste millions of dollars annually, tutoring children who are emotionally unprepared to absorb such knowledge. It is like adding more fuel to the tank of your car, when what it really needs are new sparkplugs.

In the case of the child, the intelligence may be there, but it cannot be tapped. Special assistance through tutoring only begins to be effective when the child's motivation can be directed toward the concept of learning and acquiring knowledge. So long as this is not the case, all the tutor's good work may remain no more than an unheard monologue.

I have known children with emotional learning disabilities, however, who have made excellent progress with the help of tutors, provided these have had considerable insight into the child's emotional makeup. Under fortunate circumstances, a particular tutor will do wonders for a particular child for particular reasons. While a tutor's personality makeup and insight may be only slightly relevant to the teaching needs of a normal child, in the child with emotionally-caused underachievement the selection and qualities of the right tutor become vital considerations. In other words, a sympathetic and sensitive tutor, working in collaboration with both parent and therapist, can help the child make valuable strides.

Frequently, learning difficulties stem from external causes, having little to do with the child's own personality and emotional makeup. Such cases can indeed be puzzling. School performance may be poor, even though achievement tests may indicate a quite satisfactory performance. Bill, an eighteen-year-old high school senior, is a case in point. His I.Q. was 128. His achievement tests showed him to be beyond his age level. Nonetheless, he was failing in most subjects. In therapy, Bill revealed that he was tense and deeply concerned about his parents' marriage, which seemed headed for the rocks. He felt himself partly to blame, since his parents had always fought over him. Here is a case where the boy was perfectly capable of performing his schoolwork, but his ability was severely interfered with by his consuming concern over his parents' marriage.

Family stress can often impose severe handicaps on otherwise normally functioning children. Some of these externally caused pressures, if removed, leave no permanent marks. Children under such circumstances quite easily return to a high level of learning performance. It is significant in Bill's case that while tutoring seemed of little avail during this period, the same tutor performed absolute miracles once it became quite clear to Bill that his parents' marriage ties were considerably more secure than their frequent bickering would have indicated. Bill's parents realized that their own relationship with each other had much to do with their son's backwardness. They reacted to this challenge with great understanding and diligence and fully cooperated with the therapist.

This brings us to the major point of parental support. Some parents feel understandably stymied and baffled by such learning breakdowns. I doubt very much that any other form of emotional distress in the child can prove as deeply frustrating. The more the parent tries to induce learning, the less it may be realized.

How then can parents help? Some general guidelines on how a suspected learning disorder may be approached may be helpful. Your first step, of course, is basic to all else: Once you suspect that your child is beginning to encounter school difficulties, go to the school without delay. Whatever the problem, it will not be solved by ignoring it. Do not wait for the school to sound the alarm.

Most teachers are very much aware of learning disorders. They are understanding listeners. But their interest in your child is by necessity diluted by the many children in their charge, and it may very well be up to you to make the first move.

If the school does not feel the learning disability to be serious, it is best to follow their advice on how the problem should be handled. The school wants and needs the parents' cooperation. They will appreciate your early interest and your intelligent support. Sometimes, school authorities may feel that a slightly adjusted home life is all that is needed to correct a relatively minor learning disability. Calmer meal-times, less parental pressures (or more), a change in the general household routine, can under certain circumstances contribute substantially. Such adjustments represent a very small price indeed for helping your youngster get a sound start toward his school and life career.

I often tell parents that there are three commandments in regard to a child's learning disability which one ought to adhere to diligently: The first is Cooperation. This entails free and intelligent cooperation with the school authorities, as well as with your child along the lines which seem best under a given set of circumstances.

Patience the second commandment requires perhaps a few additional comments. Learning disabilities may take as long to depart as they took to develop. It must be quite obvious by now that we deal here with complex and deep-seated emotional disturbances. If they are to be solved at all, they will be solved gradually. Patience, while exceedingy difficult to maintain when one's own youngster falls back ever further, is nonetheless required in ample measure.

I don't believe that Alertness requires much discussion. The opposite of alertness is Apathy. Many parents fall into the easy trap of believing their children will outgrow their learning disabilities. If such disabilities are emotionally caused, growing older, I am afraid, provides no solution to a learning disability. Constant alertness to the changing patterns of this difficulty, on the other hand, can do much to contribute to an early solution. While I have already said that some learning disabilities are extremely difficult to correct, the fact that the parent is properly cued in on the child's emotional pattern stands very much in the child's favor.

Only too often we encounter otherwise intelligent parents who for some reason or another refuse to recognize that a learning problem exists. I recall urging the parents of a thirteen-year-old boy to seek psychiatric help, because all symptoms indicate a clear-cut case of underachievement in a very bright youngster. Each time Charles would fail a course, his authoritarian father would add another form of punishment to an already long list of severe disciplinary actions. Diagnostic tests on Charles at the time showed a severe schizoid disturbance and a very decided, if silent, hatred for his father.

The parents, however, refused all help. Instead, Charles was placed in an academic private school for underachievers. Now Charles is eighteen, unable to enter any college because of his total inability to meet even minimum college entrance requirements. Wtih proper therapeutic help for both Charles and his parents, Charles probably could have overcome his learning disability. He could have been ready for college. But five years of in-decision lowered the boom on this boy's future.

With full parental support, the story, however, can turn out quite differently. John was the highly gifted son of a high-powered intellectual family. The drive for intellectual achievement was so in-tense that John had to make the choice of either being first in his class or risking the intense dis-approval of his parents. John's work began to deteriorate and his anxiety began to build up. He convinced himself that it might be better to fail by not trying, rather than to do his very best and then be found wanting by his parents.

Happily, we were able to solve John's problems by working directly with his parents. By assuring them that their son was worth loving whether he was first or last in his class, they succeeded in removing all of his inner anxiety. Johnny began to function once more with perfect equanimity and self-assurance. In the end, he turned out to be not at the top of his class, but he came very close to it.

How do clinics and therapists help a child's learning disorder? The first service a clinic can perform far better than the parent, of course, is professional diagnosis. At the first hint of a learn-ing disability, a series of diagnostic tests will in most cases provide sufficient insight into the seriousness and nature of the problem. Diagnostics will also help determine the type of treatment needed.

A therapeutic relationship in itself often affords great support for a child with emotional problems. If the therapist can "reach" the child, such ses-sions help reduce emotional tensions and will re-lease sufficient emotional energy for the learning process.

If and when such a relationship is established, the therapist can move ahead on many fronts. He can begin to interpret to the child the motivations of his own behavior. The skilled therapist will soon enough explain the child back to himself, interpret the child's feelings to his parents, and the parents' own emotions to the child. If the therapeutic relationship continues to be successful, the child's fantasy will sooner or later meld into reality, while his anxiety turns into a more accurate self-assessment.

This is one of the ways in which learning problems can be solved. It presupposes a close relationship between the therapist and the child. This is often difficult when a learning disorder is involved. Passive children—who are often children with learning disorders—only involve themselves with great difficulty, and the therapist is apt to be quite unsuccessful in reaching the inner resources of the child. Children with such learning problems may comply superficially, but the results of such therapy often remain disappointing.

Many, if not most, child guidance centers also offer remedial reading services, which can frequently be applied with good success. Remedial reading forces the child to focus on reality and thus reduces his opportunity to day-dream. It has other advantages also. Remedial reading offers the child a further relationship of some substance, and helps the child focus on a given area of interest. All of this forms a pattern of therapy which may contribute to some amelioration of learning and reading disabilities.

In trying to assay potential learning disabilities at an early age, some mention should also be made of the relationship of the learning function to related developmental processes. The ability to learn will in large measure depend upon the speed of the child's over-all maturation. A child will not be ready to begin reading in any true sense of the term until his perceptual and motor, as well as conceptual, performance has reached a given level. Reading readiness, in other words, is a function of over-all development. The normal child with a well-developed ability to coordinate cerebral and motor functions, who has a sense of space and relationships, is not likely to encounter a reading problem. But if these abilities are for some reason impeded or delayed, learning at even the kindergarten level may be pushing the child beyond his ability to cope with new learning tasks.

Eventual trouble at school can never be predicted with any sense of accuracy, nor does the total prevention of such difficulties come packaged in some magic formula. Were we to understand more fully the multiple causations of learning disorders, the prevention and cure would prove far easier.

One is struck, however, by the frequency with which learning disorders are tied to a particular kind of home environment. Since the basic parent-child relationship is so often involved in the development of learning problems, we should do all we can to enhance this relationship. Parents do most to avoid reading and learning problems when they can provide a stable marriage, sound human instincts, a good home environment, the encouragement of intellectual curiosity without overbearing pressures, the reward for learning achievements, and the acceptance and channeling of childhood aggressions.

The key to avoiding many learning problems is the deceptively simple one of parental love and attention. Where home circumstances are not fortuitous, children for a number of reasons may become permanently handicapped and thus lead a half-functioning and often distorted life. Children out of underprivileged homes, for these reasons, have a particularly difficult time in this regard. Children who cannot read well are more likely to drop out of school and are more likely to turn into delinquents.

The process begins early. In a psychology laboratory at the University of Chicago, for example, underprivileged four-year-olds are being fed a balanced diet of love and instruction to provide them with something they do not get at home "For such children," says Dr. Fred L. Strodtbeck, director of this study, "love and patience—given at this early age—may be the most important step in helping the child learn from teachers."

For the child who for some reason must get back at the world, who is afraid of acquiring new knowledge, or who sees himself with the distorted image of total failure, the act of someone caring still remains the best antidote.

The failure in school is often a much broader failure of life. These can be tragedies of immeasurable proportions, exceeded only by the parents' failure to provide the love and understanding which should be in every human heart to give.

1 "Fathers of Sons with Primary Neurotic Learning Inhibitions," Gruenbaum et al., *American Journal of Orthopsychiatry*, Vol. XXXII, No. 3, p. 462-472.

XII

Getting Help:
When, Where, and How

SEEKING OUTSIDE PROFESSIONAL HELP for your child is never a simple decision. It is rarely easy to find, and the results are not always fraught with success. On the other hand, it may be absolutely essential that you as the parent must make just such a decision, no matter what the inconvenience, the emotional turmoil, or the prospects of success or failure.

The first major decision, of course, is the most basic of all: Does your child really need outside help? This book has dealt repeatedly with the dangers of letting things slide too long, rather than taking a preventive approach at the first hint of some deep emotional difficulty. One also needs to be reminded, however, that all too many adults rely on psychiatry as they would a crutch, and often for reasons which are clinically unsupportable. People sometimes choose psychiatrists in lieu of priests, ministers, or rabbis. Therapists make ideal outlets for weeping hearts, for cathartic outpourings of frustrations, when all that is really needed is for the person involved to lead a more useful life.

I mention such cases since some parents send children to treatment centers in pure and simple abdication of their own responsibilities and not because their child suffers from some acute emotional problem.

The number of parents who needlessly ask for help for their children, however, is far outweighed by parents who should seek help and do not. Parents frequently postpone such decisions from one year to the next. Many have only the faintest idea as to what is involved, what are the methods used in diagnosis and treatment, what kinds of facilities are available, what are the costs of treatment, and what therapeutic results they may hope to expect.

Judging from the frequent talks I give to parents' groups, I am convinced that this whole process of seeking psychiatric help for children rests heavily on many a parent's mind. In our own profession, we also do a good deal of worrying, and parents need to be aware of this as well. We worry about the appalling lack of facilities for child therapy, and about the astonishing number of children who should have treatment, but do not get it for one reason or another.

Indeed, to us in psychiatry, our sorely strained treatment resources are a matter of growing professional and social concern. To the parent in search of help, this situation often translates itself almost immediately into a waiting list of months or even years, or forces them to seek facilities far beyond their financial reach.

Fortunately, there is at last a growing awareness of the national need to improve radically our mental health facilities. It is in my opinion a sad comment that a nation which has out-produced out-purchased, out-provided every other country on the globe has done so little and so late. Of every dollar spent on medical research, considerably less than ten cents goes into the mental aspects of illness. We have 180,000 doctors, but only 11,000 physicians in psychiatry. We have several million emotionally disturbed children, but only 500 certified child psychiatrists.

No wonder that many of our best guidance clinics and treatment facilities are now being strained to the breaking point. In my own clinic, for example, we are six months behind in our case load. For the parent, this means that half a year is needed to clear up our backlog before we can see families who apply today. Waiting lists such as these are typical of child guidance clinics everywhere. We do not always adhere to a first-come, first-served basis, but give priority to the most serious and immediately urgent cases.

The problem is further abetted by the months and years of procrastination and indecision on the part of parents. Children are totally dependent on their parents for recognizing symptoms of disturbed behavior, and obtaining appropriate help to treat the difficulty. Children, after all, cannot cry out for themselves. They cannot themselves analyze the underlying causes for their bed-wetting or their compulsive rituals. They can only act out what they feel, either consciously or unconsciously. They trust their parents to provide solace and a comforting hand when their world seems to come apart.

Preventive treatment of the emotionally disturbed child is invariably more successful when begun at the earliest possible stage. If a book such as this serves any significant purpose, it is that it may help parents to stay alert to the early warning signs of disturbed behavior. In childhood, the distinctions between what appears to be normal and abnormal behavior are at times tissue-thin. But even then the evidence is abundantly clear, many parents fail to act to protect their child as well as themselves.

Much of the parents' hesitation is due to their lack of confidence in themselves. Many adult insecurities, after all, are bound up in this business of parenthood. The parent often fears his own involvement. In therapy, however, this very involvement can be a most positive one. From the very first hour with a parent, I impress upon him or her the fact that no psychiatric treatment will ever substitute for the unique love, affection, and care by each parent for each child. Without parental support and reinforcement, child therapy only rarely proves successful. Parents, in other words, represent the backbone of the child's world. If this breaks or is denied, the child's world, too, disintegrates. Therapy helps to reconstruct the child's world, and helps both him and his parents put things into proper focus.

Once parents decide that their youngster needs outside help, their biggest hurdle is behind them. This "moment of truth" is the recognition that the child's disturbance is not a parental failure, but rather represents his distorted view of reality and a rational world. Parents invariably gain from the effects of therapy. I know many mothers and fathers who at an early stage would have used any excuse to miss an appointment with the therapist, but who now show up not only punctually, but gladly. Initial sessions, to be sure, are often less than an unalloyed success. Last-minute cancellations of appointments annotate my appointment calendar. Fears of uncovering long-locked family skeletons bring some parents to call in incredible excuses. The daughter of one frightened mother I have treated has had suspected chicken pox three times, while another little girl develops a curious

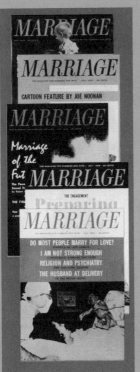

kind of allergy about an hour before each treatment session.

Neither chicken pox nor allergy was the culprit. The culprit was fear: the fear, for instance, that therapy may reveal a ghastly succession of family tales and human failures. The therapist's function, of course, is quite the opposite: his is not to blame, but to understand. Not to judge, but to listen, to guide and to encourage true emotional expression. The therapist seeks to help and heal the hurt in both the child and the parent. While it is the child who is brought in for treatment, the parents' suffering can be equally severe, and both parents must be considered an integral and essential part of treatment.

Some parents are inclined to shift the entire burden of helping their youngster onto the therapist. Forty-five minutes of weekly therapy is hardly sufficient emotional nutrition for a child with a troubled heart and mind. Parents must never assume that the introduction of a therapist into the picture relieves them of parental responsibilities. The child's emotional environment, never the therapy alone will cure him. Child therapy is essentially "family-oriented" therapy.

A corporation executive I know tries to schedule a number of therapeutic sessions for his disturbed daughter whenever he cannot give her time at home. Unhappily, the elimination of a girl's emotional pains cannot be bought or buried by the clock.

What is often overlooked is the fact that the primary cause of most childhood disturbance does not stem from the child. It comes from the emotionally charged relationship between parent and child. Healing the child's emotional wounds must normally involve healing of the bonds between parent and child. Without the parents' full cooperation, prospects of getting to the root of the matter are much diminished.

What, then, is a parent to do, when he has reached his own "moment of truth"? Under most circumstances, a number of possibilities exist. All should be explored by both parents, although not yet with the child. Initial consultations should always be confined to the parents and the professional, with the child being drawn in later on.

How to find help, and what kind? Consulting your own family physician is often a good first step. While not equipped to perform therapy himself, your physician is apt to be more aware than you of facilities in your area. Seeing your doctor first will also help him assess any possible physical basis for your child's troubled behavior.

Your school may be another excellent source of referral. An increasing number of schools retain guidance counselors, either on their staff or as consultants. Most keep well informed on community facilities. Additionally, your minister, priest, or rabbi can probably give you sensible counsel. He may also provide helpful information about community child guidance clinics, especially those that are church-related.

Your telephone book is also a good starting point. Check the listing for "Mental Health Associations," and you may well be on your way to finding what you need. Several national organizations can also be helpful to you in a number of ways. The National Association of Mental Health, Inc. (10 Columbus Circle, New York, N.Y. 10019) lists nine hundred local chapters. An inquiry will bring you the address of their state division, which in turn will guide you to your local chapter.

The American Association of Psychiatric Clinics

for Children (250 West 57th Street, New York, N.Y.) will provide the name of an accredited member-clinic if there is one in your area.

Should you prefer a psychiatric social worker, write to the National Association of Social Workers (2 Park Avenue, New York, N.Y.) and request a list of their chapter chairman. They in turn can advise you on nearby qualified members. Members must have at least a master's degree in social work, with extensive training in psychotherapy. Members of the Academy of Certified Social Workers have an additional two years of supervised experience.

Other telephone listings may help. Look for the Community Chest, the United Fund, Council for Social Agencies, your local medical society, your local college (Department of Psychology or Medicine), or the staff of your local hospital. Your medical society and hospital may also be able to refer you to a practicing psychiatrist. Not many psychiatrists, however, undertake treatment of children. This should be determined before an appointment is made.

An additional reliable contact point may be your local Family Service Agency. It has wide representation in many parts of the nation. An increasing number of local chapters offer diagnostic testing facilities as well as psychiatric services and child guidance. Even where they do not do so themselves, Family Service Agencies are a good source of advice as to where and what kind of child guidance services may be available in your community.

One word of caution. In the field of community psychological services, all is not gold that glitters. Quacks and pseudo-experts with fancy names abound in this area of medicine as in others. Parents are well advised not to measure professionl competence by impressive labels, with which some tend to advertise themselves.

A now very unhappy and considerably poorer mother comes to mind, who spent a small fortune on her anxiety-ridden boy at a certain clinic, at which the major forms of therapy consisted of a stereophonic record player with "therapeutic mood music" and an exercise device designed to rid the boy of "inner tensions." These devices were rented out at a high price for home use, and claimed to bring therapy into the living room. One is always astonished at the ingenuity of such schemes and the gullibility of people who succumb to them.

The best assurance parents can have of securing professional services is to seek out facilities which are recognized by one of the professional associations mentioned earlier. I would advise parents to judge similarly the reputation of individual psychotherapists and analysts. There staff connections will readily indicate their own professional attainment. When they are attached to a recognized clinic or similar treatment facilities, parents can rest assured that their professionalism and training are unquestioned.

Once parents have located a suitable and reputable clinic or an individual therapist, setting up an appointment is the obvious next step. The first interview is of particular significance for a number of reasons. Many parents, in my experience, would feel less uneasy if they were better informed as to what to expect and the arrangement usually involved.

In my own clinic, which is typical, the procedure goes something like this: The parents call for an interview. The clinic determines an appointment convenient to both parties. The first interview, of course, may not be scheduled immediately. Much depends on the particular clinic's schedule and staff availability at the time of the parents' first inquiry. Parents are asked to come without their child. The interview (or "intake," as we refer to it) is conducted by a psychiatric social worker. Within the first forty-five-minute session, the therapist attempts to determine just what the parents view their child's basic problem to be. If this is impossible to ascertain in one session, a second session is scheduled.

In addition to this joint conference, the mother and father may be asked to return individually for further discussions with the therapist. There are family circumstances where discussions with one parent alone may reveal dynamics and relationships significant to the eventual diagnosis, but which he or she may express only when alone.

Asking one parent to return alone may be disturbing to both parents. But absolute privacy of communications represents one of psychiatry's vital professional pillars. Discretion is part of all psychiatric practice. I think it is important for parents to remember that whatever may be said between themselves and the psychiatric clinician and therapist cannot be revealed even to their own doctor, school officials, or cleric, without the express permission of the parties involved.

What is the general purpose and intent of such diagnostic sessions? Diagnostic services generally fall into set patterns. The first phase revolves on a summary report by the therapist to his clinical team. Typical of this first phase is a series of four interviews: the first is held with the parents, the second and third with the mother and father individually, the fourth with the child.

In our joint conference with both parents, we

try to trace the entire development of the child. We go back as far as we can. We ask questions. Many questions. What were the conditions of the marriage before the child's birth? Was the infant wanted, was it planned for, or were some other circumstances involved?

What of the pregnancy? How did the mother feel about it? Were there complications? What about the birth itself? Was labor prolonged? Was anesthesia used? Instruments? How would they describe the baby's condition during the first six weeks? Was it overactive, underactive, did it eat and sleep normally? Was it breast-fed or bottle-fed? If bottle-fed was is propped up or was the baby cuddled and held during feeding periods?

When and how was the child weaned? When did he walk and when did he talk? What about his toilet-training, when and how was it accomplished? What illnesses can you recall since his birth, what accidents, what hospitalization, and, what was his emotional reaction? Any other traumatic events? What is the emotional environment of the child, as seen in relation to his parents, his brothers and sisters, his playmates, his school, cub-scout troop, his grandfather, step father?

Our questions, of course, are not confined to the child alone. Questions are addressed to the parents as well. Preferably in individual interviews, we try to ascertain the general character of the family's emotional history, record vital family events and crisses, make some objective judgments in terms of relationships to the grandparents and other key family members. In short, we aim for an accurate diagnostic profile of the whole family. The more distinctly we can draw such a picture, the better the clinic is equipped to make its recommendations.

While the parents are thoroughly interviewed, the child's school authorities are asked for certain information in regard to the child's general school performance and behavior. Such school impressions frequently reveal a good deal.

Then the child is seen alone. We do what we can to make his or her first encounter as relaxing and nonthreatening as possible. Children, of course, react in different ways. I can assure parents that such sessions do not resemble the first encounter with the dentist. The atmosphere is relaxed. It will probably strike the child to be without purpose. He is not talked to, but talked with. The difference is telling. If this first visit were to strike the child as some form of inquisition, the purpose of subsequent therapy would be dangerously underminded.

With the completion of this first series of sessions, the therapist summarizes his observations, and, together with the results of the school questionnaire in hand, forwards his or her diagnostic impressions to the clinic's staff psychiatrist. The psychiatrist reviews the case and asks for psychological and psychiatric evaluations. Broadly speaking, three categories of tests are involved: this includes an I.Q. test, personality tests, and a Bender-Gestalt test to establish possible organic damage.

Once these tests have been completed and evaluated by the psychologist, the child and both parents are individually seen by the clinic psychiatrist. By now the psychiatrist has gained his own impressions. Now he joins the clinic psychologist and psychiatric social worker for an over-all evaluation to determine diagnosis and recommendations.

The purpose of such a staff conference is to reach conclusions in these general areas:

1. Is the child disturbed or is he not?

2. Are his disturbances of such a nature that they can be treated in an outpatient clinic? Or is the case so serious and in need of immediate intensive attention that hospitalization or residential treatment should be recommended?

3. Are both parents and child sufficiently motivated to take advantage of psychiatric help?

4. What is the tentative diagnosis? Can some prognosis be given?

5. What treatment plans can be decided upon?

This staff conference concludes the diagnostic phase. All that remains is for the parent to consult once again with the psychiatric social worker, during which session the staff findings are interpreted and future action, if any, is recommended.

Acceptance or rejection of the clinic's recommendations are, of course, for the parents to make. Obviously, one always hopes, for the sake of the child, that the clinic's recommendations are accepted. Parents naturally await the results of the diagnostic study with a good deal of concern. To anticipate the unknown is always difficult. When the happiness of your own child is involved, such uncertainties can be particularly trying. Parental apprehension is understandable, but only rarely justified by the facts. I am inclined to say, in fact, that many parents who worry, need not; and those who do not worry, should.

Of all the children who come to us for diagnostics, some require no help whatsoever. A larger number are helped by relatively short-term counseling with both child and parents, while still another large segment benefits substantially by more intensive psychotherapy. Fortunately, only a very small percentage of children diagnosed are so seriously disturbed as to require immediate hospitalization or residential treatment.

The more serious the emotional disorder, the more difficult it seems for us to impress those facts upon the parents. The very seriously disturbed child, I am sorry to say, is the same child whose parents may very well refuse to see the problem in its total dimensions. In the case of the severely disturbed, the highly perturbing prognosis may seem to the untutored eye so totally out of line with the child's *apparent* behavior. To parents, this surface anomaly often becomes too difficult to comprehend.

Not long ago, I advised a father to seek immediate help for his son. His fourteen-year-old boy was so seriously disturbed that he could well make an attempt on his father's life. Both parents rejected our recommendations. They considered our diagnosis completely "ridiculous." No more than six weeks later, a call from the psychiatric unit of the state hospital confirmed what we had feared: the boy had been forcibly hospitalized after an attempted homicide of his school principal.

This experience is not uncommon. I believe that this boy could have been helped. His parents disagreed, which was their right. Such tragedies always unfold on two sides: for the parents, no more punishment can be imagined for their error of judgment. For us as well as society at large, our failure is equally appalling in terms of our inability to reduce emotional suffering.

Parents should not only seek advice from professionally equipped people, but should then follow through on advice once given. I can assure parents that I know of no responsible person or institution involved in treating the disturbed child who will advise therapy when this is not realistically called for. Aside from all professional considerations, present facilities are all too crowded to allow for any ballast of children who may require less or no help of any kind.[1]

The kind of specific help that parents must ultimately choose will depend upon the severity of their child's disturbance, and treatment facilities in terms of availability, proximity, and financial requirements. The more serious the child's problem, the narrower their possibilities of choice. For the child in need of no more than a steadying hand on the shoulder, an outside friend, a sympathetic doctor, or a family counselor with sufficient insight may do nobly.

For the child in need of more intensive psychotherapy, several kinds of organizations as well as individual professional people offer competent help. These include psychiatrists, psychoanalysts, psychologists, as well as psychotherapists. Certain childhood problems can also be helped by speech therapists and remedial teachers, often working in tandem with a child's psychotherapist.

Where is such help most likely to be obtained? Unless the child is seriously disturbed, as shown by his or her diagnostic study, one of two alternatives are recommended: the most accessible help will probably come from either a recognized outpatient child guidance clinic or a qualified child psychotherapist. In either case, typical treatment patterns call for therapy sessions once or twice weekly, with parallel, but separate, sessions with the child's parents.

If the child is found seriously disturbed, such frequency or therapy may prove insufficient. In such cases, the manifestations of severe mental disorder may leave no other choice but to place the child in some suitable inpatient residential treatment center. These are found in either specially equipped hospitals or in schools and camps set up to treat seriously disturbed children. For the child too emotionally ill to remain at home, or where a total change of environment is deemed crucial, a residential treatment center may represent the best source of treatment possible. One of the best examples of exceptional staff and facilities for the seriously disturbed child are the Devereux Schools in Pennsylvania, California, and Texas. In these schools, a highly trained professional staff devotes months and often years to curing or at least helping emotionally handicapped youngsters, each receiving expert and intensive psychiatric care.

Crucial to the very success of therapy is the degree with which the child can relate to his therapist. In contrast to most adults, children, depending on their age, verbalize poorly. The normal means available in adult therapy would never form a good communicating link between child and therapist.

For this reason the therapist may use various forms of play therapy as a treatment tool. Especially with pre-puberty children, the expression of their fantasies is most effectively conveyed by the use of dollhouses, family figures, and puppets. These act as a catalyst for the child to express and work out his problems. The free use of aggressive toys such as guns, toy soldiers, and punching bags is also employed for clinical insight, as well as for cathartic purposes.

With each succeeding session, most children will display ever freer forms of expressions and associations. The therapist helps the child act out his fears, depressions, and anxieties, and helps him see for himself the distinctions between his own fantasies and the realities of life.

Once we help the child bridge these often strident gaps between his inner self and outer world of reality, such self-recognition is usually followed by increasingly normal and rational behavior patterns. With some children, I regret to say, the facts of their outer world may be more devastating than the idyllic reveries of their own minds. The horror of some child's inner fantasies is only too often matched by the harsh realities of his existence. Whatever the treatment situation, the role of the therapist is that of a neutral sounding board, allowing and gently encouraging the child to express his real feelings. These exasperations can include fear, aggression, hate, or alternate displays of extreme affection, clinging dependency, or an intense jealousy of the therapist's concern with other children. The whole spectrum of such emotions can be displayed by the same child within a single forty-five-minute session.

The relationship between therapist and child is a carefully controlled and studied situation. The child's emotional variations, his ups and downs, the depths and heights, are always measurable against the stable constancy of the therapist's own neutrality. The therapist interprets and plays back to the child his own attitudes and feelings toward himself and the people of his own world. Once the therapist succeeds in establishing a satisfactory relationship (sometimes the child's first), the child's emotional capacity for meaningful human relationships will most likely be considerably enhanced. In short, the therapist tries through psychotherapy to bring the child's unconscious mechanisms to the surface, by projecting them through play, art forms, and, of course, verbal interplay between therapist and patient. In time, successful therapy will result in the child's growing awareness of his deeper emotional problems, from which can then emerge better ways of dealing with them.

What about the financial cost? Answers to this question depend upon so many variables as to make generalizations difficult. Child therapy may not only be of long duration, but may need to be maintained at a high rate of intensity. Effective therapy is never achieved when treatment is erratic and occasional. A systematic schedule of treatment hours and the continuous cooperation by the family are necessary ingredients toward terminating treatment successfully.

The least expensive form of treatment for the less seriously disturbed child is apt to be a community clinic. Fees are customarily scaled according to the family's ability to pay. Typical of the formula applied is that of my own clinic, where weekly fees are assessed at 1 percent of the family's federal income tax. If, for example, a family's tax payment last year came to $800, the clinic's weekly charge for all members of the family would be set at $8.00. Should the fee reach $15.00, the family would be referred to a private clinic or a private therapist.

Private practitioners, of course, can provide greater flexibility of treatment hours and conditions than overcrowded clinics. Private psychotherapists, psychiatrists, psychoanalysts, and clinical psychologists set their own fees, which may range from a minimum of $10.00 per session to $50.00. There again, fees are determined with some flexibility, much depending upon the patient's financial capacity.

When the emotional illness is severe, costs can easily skyrocket. Just as in the case of major surgery, chronic physical ailments, or orthodontia, treatment of the severely disturbed child can run into thousands of dollars. For the few who can afford it, a small private hospital may charge as much as $1,000 a month or more. Psychiatric sections of general hospitals will charge considerably less. State hospitals represent the only alternative open to many people, but the quality of their services, with a few exceptions, rarely equals that of custodial care. State hospitals are therefore rarely bargains in terms of this discussion. A schizophrenic child may be charged $60.00 a month in a well-equipped and well-staffed state hospital and only $10.00 or $20.00 in a poorly equipped one. But he may be releasable in the first case in less than a year, while he may languish for much of his life in a low-cost, custodial care hospital without any marked improvement. The mathematics can be as simple as that.

There are signs that at least some part of the cost of psychiatric care will in the future be borne by an ever larger number of health insurance plans. Some private group insurance plans as well as current Blue Shield plans already cover certain psychiatric services in hospitals, while some private plans now extend into home as well as office psychiatric treatment.

Some parents become concerned about the basis of hourly charges. Rates for therapy are based on individual sessions, which may range from forty-five to fifty minutes each. Parents should feel free to clarify this point of duration with their clinic or private practitioner before treatment is begun. A forty-five- or fifty-minute treatment hour is quite typical, allowing the therapist ten to fifteen minutes for his own review of each case and the required annotation for his clinical records. If the therapist spends two consecutive forty-five-minute sessions with a child, parents will be billed for the one and a half hours on the basis of two sessions. Similarly, clinics and therapists charge the agreed-upon rate for all services performed on behalf of the child, including school visitations, family consultations, as well as professional conferences with the family doctor. Permission from the parent is invariably obtained beforehand.

There are no bargain prices in the cure of emotional illness. Even a mildly disturbed child may require weekly therapy sessions over the course of an entire year. Total annual cost may range from several hundred to one thousand dollars and up. But no price tag can be put on stabilizing a child's emotionality, nor on averting in many cases more serious and permanent psychic damage. Many parents I know forego some hope for luxuries to make such treatment possible. Vacations, a new car, or summer camp, may need to fall by the wayside. Most do it gladly. Others balance one against the other, and opt for the luxuries instead of the child. It is a view of life which says much about the parents involved.

If the cost of therapy can be high, what of its rewards? One of the great frustrations of psychiatry is that human emotionality does not lend itself to computerized formulas. Psychotherapy counts its failures along with its successes. But by whatever means it is measured, a number of studies on the effects of psychotherapy show that evidence of substantial improvement is present in at least two-thirds of all cases. Such percentages are considerably enhanced when the child receives prolonged therapy, when such treatment is begun early enough, and when both parents are involved wholeheartedly.

The main goal of child therapy is not total cure of the child's problems, but the gaining of sufficient insight to help him successfully handle feelings such as anger, hostility, and anxiety. Much of child therapy is prophylactic, while other aspects are concerned with compensating for specific emotional handicaps. A patient with a crippled left hand will develop greater strengths in his right. Similarly, the child with an emotional propensity to anxiety can, once understood, readjust by his very awareness of his problem. Effective therapy removes the veils of irrationality that may enshroud the child, and helps him throw light on himself with a clearer vision and a firmer heart.

Most important, parents must not expect improvement according to some set schedule. Two steps forward may well be followed by one step back. The child of today is not the child of yesterday, nor will tomorrow be like today. As a parent you must also know that the only constancy of childhood is the pulse of a changing and emerging personality. Problems change too. One measure of the effectiveness of therapy is the child's ability to cope with each change as it comes along.

Above all, parents should have this branded upon their uppermost consciousness: their child's inner self is not the haphazard result of supernatural and uncontrollable forces, but the sum total of life experiences, to which the mother and father are its chief contributors.

Your child's inner world does not play out its scenes in some distant and disembodied place. Its main setting is your own heart and soul. These engage his individuality and shape the inner world of this precious human being. He is your child.

He is worth your most tender love, the limits of your strength, and the very depth of your understanding.

1 An excellent summary on the subject of professional help is contained in a booklet, *When Children Need Special Help with Emotional Problems*. Address request and forty cents to Child Study Association of America, Inc., 9 East 89th Street, New York, N.Y.

INDEX

Index